पुरातत्त्व

PURĀTATTVA

Bulletin of the Indian Archaeological Society

No. 17 1986-87

Editor

S.P. Gupta

D.K. Printworld (P) Ltd.
New Delhi

Cataloging in Publication Data — DK
[Courtesy : D.K. Agencies (P) Ltd. <docinfo@dkagencies.com>]

Purātattva : bulletin of the Indian Archaeological
Society, no. 17, 1986-87 / editor, S.P. Gupta.
p. cm.
Includes bibliographical references.
ISBN 8124602921

1. Archaeology — India — Periodicals. 2. India
— Antiquities — Periodicals. 3. India — Civilization
— Periodicals. I. Gupta, S.P. (Swarajya Prakash),
1931 - II. Indian Archaeological Society.

DDC 934 21

First Published in 1988
First Reprinted in 2005
ISBN 81-246-0292-1
Price for volume 17 (1986-87): Rs. 800 US $ 40

Reprint authorised by
Indian Archaeological Society
New Delhi - 110 016

The Editors are not responsible for the opinions expressed by the Contributors.

Purātattva is published annually.

Manuscripts (whether in the form of articles or notes or book reviews) offered for publication should be sent to the Editor, Purātattva, Indian Archaeological Society, B-17, Qutab Institutional Area, New Delhi - 110 016.

Published and printed by:
D.K. Printworld (P) Ltd.
'*Srikunj*,' F-52, Bali Nagar
New Delhi - 110015
Phone : (011) 2545 3975, 2546 6019 Fax : (011) 2546 5926
E-mail : dkprintworld@vsnl.net
www. dkprintworld.com

PURATATTVA

CONTENTS

NOTES AND NEWS

BOOK REVIEWS

PURATATTVA

Number 17 1986-87

Editorial

The present issue of *Puratttava* covers a wide range of subjects encompassing prehistory, protohistory and history besides art. Our aim this year was to present to our readers evidence from new archaeological excavations and explorations. In this endeavour we have been successful in that the first five articles deal with excavations and explorations. Information regarding the Copper Hoard implements collection of the National Museum, New Delhi, has been updated and here the serial numbers are the continuation from the previous article on the same subject published in *Puratattva* No. 16.

A word about the numbering of the plates: the first numeral in bold represents the article number in this issue while the succeeding one represents the number of the illustration.

The Editor and the Society offer their deep and heartfelt condolences to the bereaved family of Prof. V. A. Narayan of the Department of History, Patna University, on his untimely demise. We also mourn the death of Dr H. Sarkar, former Jt. Director General, Archaeological Survey of India. Both of them were closely associated with the activities of the Society.

The Editor and the Society are extremely beholden to the Director General, Archaeological Survey of India, New Delhi, for his timely and munificent financial grant for bringing out this issue of *Puratattva.*

The Editor also regrets any printing and other errors that may have crept in, in spite of his best efforts.

The Editor is thankful to Shri K. S. Ramachandran and Shri Ganesh Rao for their help and assistance in editing and seeing the Bulletin through the press.

Thanks are due Messrs. Navchetan Press (P) Ltd. for printing in such a short time.

S. P. GUPTA

1

Sanghol Excavations 1987: Some New Evidences

C. Margabandhu
and
G.S. Gaur

A brief report of the excavations at Sanghol has been published in the last issue of the *Puratattva* representing the highlights of the work done in 1986. This excavation, as stated earlier, was carried out by the Excavations Branch of the Archaeological Survey of India jointly with the Department of Archaeology and Museums, Govt. of Punjab and the work was again continued for the second season, during this year.

While planning the work of excavations at Sanghol, it was evident that any piecemeal approach to the problem is bound to be unrewarding, hence due care was taken to select areas, which could be properly connected by the cultural evidence of the portion, with those from other parts of the mound and link them, chronologically by the artifactual data. In other words, the extension of the town in successive periods later, due to various factors was identified, as far as possible, and trenches were laid to obtain evidence so that the reasonable expansion of the town could be properly explained and also demarcated. At the same time, the main mound (over which is situated the present village) was continuously occupied from the earliest period, at times, very thickly and possibly lateral expansion of the settlement took place much later, during the Early historical period. This was all the more reason that necessitated the careful strategy for selecting the select areas to be probed, so that maximum evidence could be obtained.

Some important aims in this season's planning is to be emphasised. First, to further expose on a horizontal scale, the large palatial complex at Hathiwara Mound (SGL-1), already revealed in limited details earlier; secondly, to confirm the existence of the 'overlap' between the Late Harappan (with substantial "Bara" painted element in the earlier sub-phases of the period) and the subsequent cultures such as the Painted Grey Ware (not yet precisely determined owing to limited area available, in the thickly populated portion of the village) at areas of the main mound apart from those aleady excavated in the earlier season; and thirdly to understand the nature, extent and the cultural artefacts and components of the post-Kushana period and after.

In order to determine these factors in a phased manner, trenches were laid at SGL-1 in Hathiwara Mound to expose the details of the large structural complex of the Kushana Period and for the second, trenches were laid at two more new areas called SGL-6 and SGL-12 situated at extensions and periphery of the early cultures and for the post-Kushana evidence, two trenches were taken closely at SGL-8. The main trenches on top of the mound (situated in the populated area of the village) laid earlier called SGL-9 where excavations were made, was continued both horizontally, as well as vertically, right up to the earliest levels. Similar excavation was also continued to understand the Late Harappan complex and later cultures at SGL-2, on the western slopes of the mound.

An attempt has been made to place the evidence, obtained from various areas of Sanghol, locality-wise, with due emphasis on the artifacts revealed from them highlighting their significance, in the following pages.

SGL-1 (Hathiwara Mound)

Excavations exposed further the large structure, possibly a palatial complex, both on the north and eastern sides. Its extensive nature, both in plan and extent and further continuity in length does not clearly envisage any known structure or plan so far revealed from other Kushana settlements. The characteristic features so far excavated include, well built pathway or a courtyard in bricks on the outer alignment with possibly an assembly hall constructed of neatly built-brick floors, on which were circular pillars, as revealed by the circular post-holes cut on the brick-floors (Pl.1). The slightly angular nature of the pathway indicate the semi-circular characteristics in plan, but the connected brick-built floor commencing from the main wall on the western side indicate, the rectangular nature of the main complex. Considering the more or less the same level of its occurrence and its belonging to the same structural phase and also of its uniform nature of its presence, in all the trenches this appears to be a long and spacious pillared hall, possibly for congregation or for assembly. Since it is further extending to the east and the floor to the south suggests a fairly large building, but its exact nature and purpose and features are still yet to be determined. It seems to dominate the Hathiwara mound and the contour lines indicate this building was almost planned in the centre around which other structures were built.

To the south-east portion of Hathiwara, in the same group was also excavated, an interesting two contiguous rectangular cistern-like structures, built adjacent to one another, padded with brick-built platform (floor) which may be a ritualistic complex (*Hawan Kunda*) or a part of a temple or possibly a portion of a warehouse (Pl.2).

Another interesting Kushana house plan, in more or less complete features, has been exposed in Hathiwara, situated on its southern periphery. Part of the structure was already exposed last year and further clearance revealed a building built in brick, consisting of main entrance repersented by a brick-ramp and a side entrance from the lane, leading to a large-sized verandah or a hall, with a room directly entering to the kitchen and bath rooms and to the three living rooms in the interior (Pl.3). Towards the lane side, is the entrance which leads to a verandah and then a small room with access direct to the living rooms. What is more significant is a small brick-built drain (partly closed) which projects out on the lane side. On the outer wall of the house, it almost passes through the kitchen and the bath rooms as found on plan in the interior. Both of them are situated on the same brick-built floors, remains of which are more or less removed by later disturbance. The main courtyard connected to them is still to be excavated.

At Hathiwara in all five structural phases have been traced out with floors built of brick bats and bricks with lime coating. Two phases of a structure with connected walls were encountered. These belong to the mid-mature phase of the Kushana period.

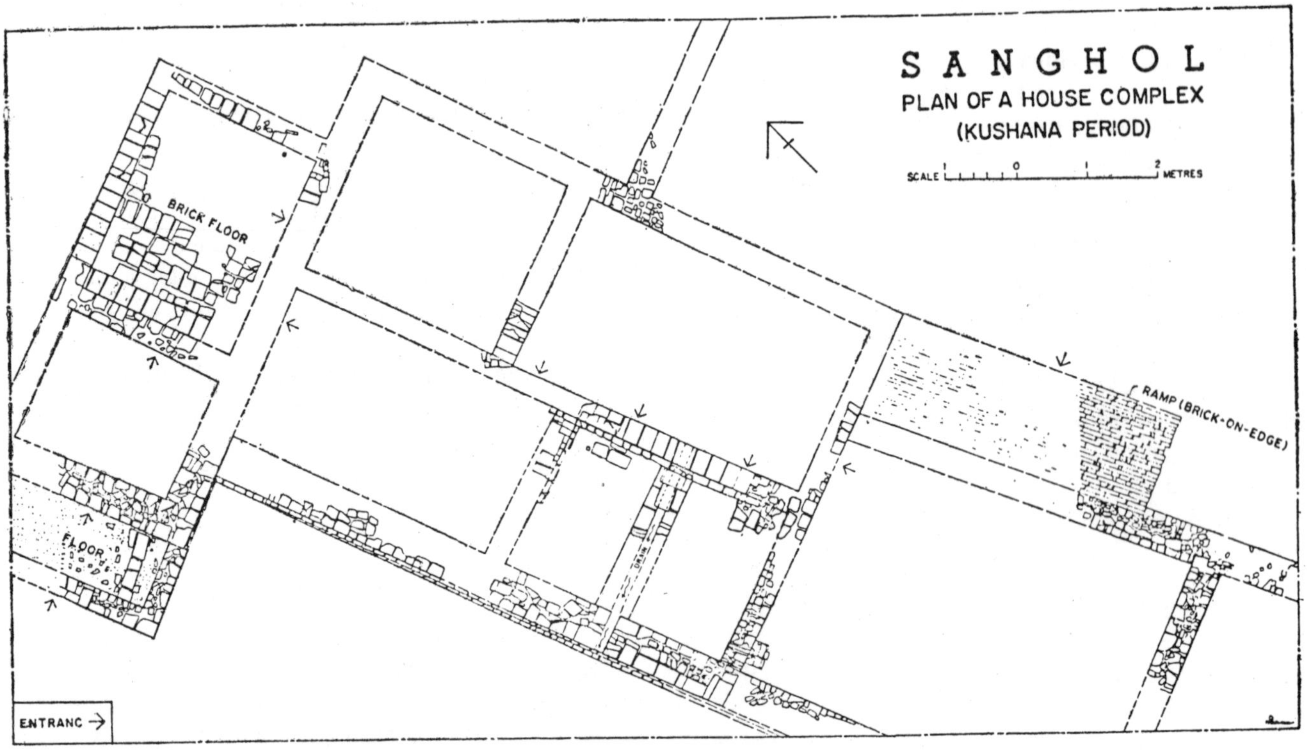

Each cistern-like structure measures 3.10 m in length, 1.36 m in width and 1.32 m in height. They were built in a continuous series (further portion is yet to be excavated) connected by burnt-brick floor and form part of a uniform plan with three offsets internally.

SGL-2

Situated on the western slopes of the mound, trenches laid earlier has been further extended which brought to light remains from the Late Harappan to the Kushana period.

Six structural phases were encountered in the Late Harappan (Bara) Period. The walls of houses were built of mud, except in Phase IV where the blocks (lumps) of mud measuring 48×40×8 cm have been used. Floors of rammed earth were also noticed. Circular corn-bins and oval *chullahas* were also exposed. The habitational layers run horizontalty revealing undisturbed levels of the settlement. Rooms were small which could accommodate three or four persons only at a time. Most of the habitational areas were built uniformly, as revealed by the horizontal layers and rooms were small and could accommodate only a few persons. The walls were built, closely connected back-to-back and they run in cardinal directions. Further, an interesting evidence of a burnt terracotta domical object on the floor was found *in situ*; the purpose of which is not clear (P1.4). Similar evidence has also been reported from many Harappan sites such as at Banawali, Ropar, Hulas, etc. Signs of burning along with ash indicate that it was fixed in position, on the floor adjacent to a side wall of the room.

Important antiquities of this period include beads of terracotta, agate and faience, circular and oval terracotta cakes, faience and terracotta bangles, terracotta wheels and balls.

Following the Bara culture (Period-I) comes the 'overlap' phase in which Late Harappan pottery, Black slipped and plain grey ware were found. The dominance of the Bara pottery was also perceptible. However, in the chronological horizon of the P.G.W. the Black slipped ware is found in abundance indicating contemporaneity of Bara and P.G.W. people.

Early Historical Period

Though not much evidence is available, this period is characterised by ceramics dominated by red ware. The structures were built of large sized mud and burnt bricks and are mainly pre-Kushana in character. Notable antiquities include beads of semi-precious stones and terracotta and bone points.

During the Kushana Period, four structural phases represented by walls of burnt as well as mud bricks were exposed. On an average, the Kushana house comprises a kitchen two or three small rooms, storage bins, round hearths and mud-brick steps. Earlier excavation (1986) has revealed a thick cluster of houses built very close to each other revealing a portion of Kushana settlement.

SGL-9

Situated in the centre of the village, it represents the highest point of the mound and earlier excavation (1986) has revealed four structural phases of the Kushana Period. A complex of double storeyed brick building has been exposed with a courtyard and series of hearth suggesting a factory site for beads and terracottas.

The cultural sequence obtained here are under :

1. Late Harappan
2. 'Overlap' phase between Late Harappan (Bara), Painted Grey Ware(?), Grey Ware and Black slipped Ware
3. Kushana Period
4. Gupta Period and
5. The Late Medieval period.

It has to be further stressed that the exact nature of the 'overlap' phase here is to be further ascertained by exposing larger area as there appears a levelling off activity at this time of habitation. However this phase seems to have continued for a fairly long period of time. The Kushana habitation is quite rich in material artefacts as well as structural features of which more than four phases were identified. Further there seems to have been some change that occurs after the post-Kushana times. However, ceramics and other associated objects of daily use and houses built of reused bricks were found and are datable to the Gupta Period. The area continued to be occupied during the Late Medieval Period.

SGL-8

This area representing an extension of Sanghol during the post-Kushana Period, is situated to the south-east of the main mound. Excavations have exposed the cultural sequence belonging to the early Medieval, Gupta and the Kushana Periods. Earlier, this part of the mound was also excavated yielding remains of similar nature. It was mainly occupied during the Gupta period. The Kushana period was represented by pottery and objects of daily use. The area denotes the periphery of the Kushana township. A sort of transitional phase from the Kushana to the Gupta period was also noticed.

Gupta artifacts are prolific, represented mainly by Red Polished Ware, stamped pottery, kaolin ware and other associated material. A burnt-brick wall mad of reused Kushana bricks was also exposed. Early Medieval Period is also represented by pottery and a few antiquities.

SGL-6

The excavation at this locality has attested the presence of the Late Harappan (Bara) culture, followed by the 'overlap' phase which is the continuation of the Bara pottery in association with Grey ware of the PGW lineage and Black slipped ware. In the Early historical phase, the structures were built of mud and burnt bricks of fairly large size ascribable to the pre-Kushana times. Coins of the Parthian rulers were also found in the upper levels.

SGL-12

Excavations here have revealed the earliest occupation datable to the Late Harappan Period along with 'Bara' ceramics and antiquities. Though no structural evidence is available, floor remains made of rammed clay is found. The layers are horizontally laid and occupation is of a fairly long duration. Traces of erosional deposits, would perhaps indicate flooding of the area at the late stage of occupation.

So far the antiquities are concerned, they are quite rich and considerable. The range of varieties are inmense and bespeak of the artistic creativity of the age. This is all the more so, in the Kushana Period. A preliminary study reveals that during the early centuries of the Christian era, the site expanded into a large township dominated by merchantmen and economically prosperous group, who patronised various types of artistic and religious activities as revealed by numerous cultural artefacts found during excavations.

Foremost among them consists of human and animal figurines in terracotta (Pls. 5 and 6); some of them artistically made in the form of handles (Pl. 7), both modelled, as well as made from mould. Varieties of stamped designs were also found on ceramics which are too numerous to mention. They include both religious and decorative symbols on a very large scale. Some of them are motifs stamped such as yaksha (Pl. 8), which is quite unique. Notable among the animals represented include bull and monkey in various postures; apart, some bird figurines are quite realistic. Another characteristic yet dominant, type includes large number of terracotta discs—circular, square and rectangular—decorated with designs and flower motifs on one side, while on the other with some typical details representing a scene such as a warrior riding a horse, a prancing lion (Pl. 9) and various animal motifs, wheels—both plain and decorated—ear studs, toy-cart frames, skin rubbers, stamps with handles (Pl. 10), rattles, female lamp bearers, balls and other archaic type of figurines. Many typical clay tablets were found in rectangular and square shape with lines incised on them, possibly representing some sort of jewellers' weights.

Important is the shell industry which is evidenced by varieties of bangles, beads, pendants and other decorated objects, cut columella, etc. Other objects include beads and pendants of semi-precious stones, terracotta, ivory, and copper, ivory and bone objects such as bangles, decorated pieces, etc.

Acknowledgement

We acknowledge with thanks Shri L. S. Mamani, Surveyor, Shri J. S. Bisht, Modeller and Shri B. B. Sharma, Photographer, all of the Excavations Branch II, Archaeological Survey of India, Purana Qila, New Delhi for their valuable work in respect of the preparation of contour plan of Sanghol, drawings of antiquities and photographs respectively. We are also thankful to Sarvashri Kuldeep Singh Sindhu, K. K. Rishi, Gurdev Singh and Hira Singh of the Punjab State Archaeology for their active participation in the field work and for multifarious help and co-operation. Shri G. B. Sharma, Sanghol also helped during excavations by his active participation. We are grateful to the Director General, Archaeological Survey of India, New Delhi for making possible the above study and also permitting to publish it. The copyright of the photographs published rests with the Archaeological Survey of India.

2

Explorations along the Banganga River, District Bharatpur, Rajasthan

Baldev Singh Negi

Bharatpur, a district of eastern Rajasthan, is irregular quadrilateral in shape, bounded by Gurgaon district of Haryana on the north, Alwar on the west, Dholpur district of Rajasthan on the south and Mathura district of Uttar Pradesh on the east. It is located at the confluence of Ruparel and Banganga, and no perennial river flows in or around the district. The major seasonal rivers here are the Banganga, the Gambhiri and the Ruparel. The river Banganga locally known as Utgan is a tributary of the Yamuna. Entering Bharatpur at Santruk it flows in a westerly direction towards the town of Alwar and by now this has ceased to be perennial stream. During its life time it was an important river, although at present it is lost in many places near the marshyland. The dried courses of these small rivulets have been replaced by a network of modern canals. Thus, Bharatpur is characterised by fault induced alluvial basin produced by Banganga and its tributaries.

Bharatpur was a part of the Brahmavarta in the Vedic period and later of the Matsya. During the early historical period it was occupied by the Yaudheyas and by the Mevas in the medieval times.

The author carried out systematic explorations in the year 1983-84 under the village to village survey scheme along the dried bed of Banganga of Bharatpur district to ascertain its Archaeological potentiality. The results obtained are of great significance and the description of antiquities and potteries found from the thirty sites along the Banganga river bed is detailed below :

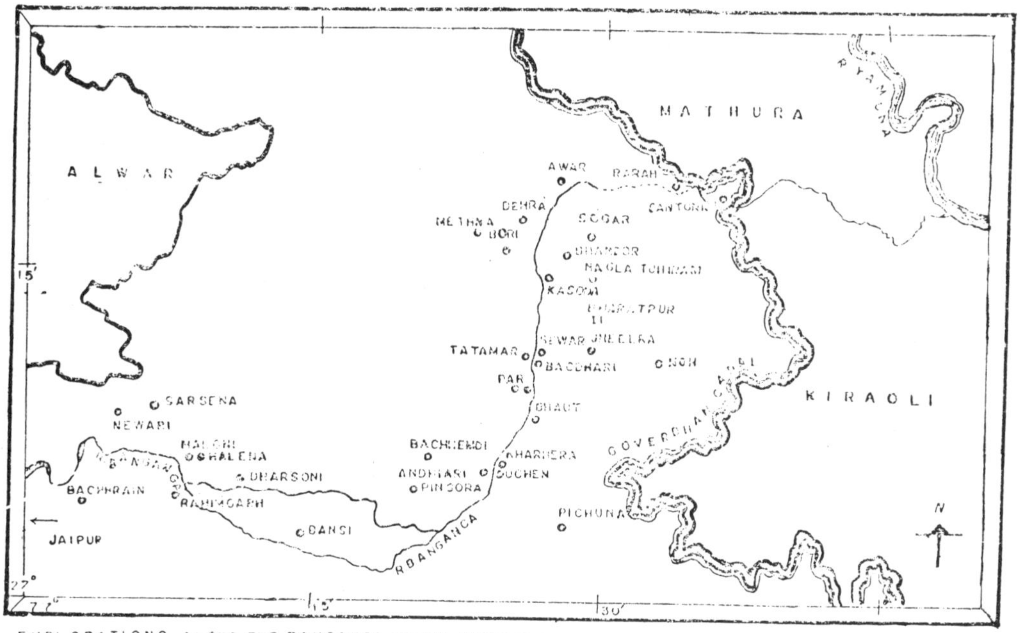

EXPLORATIONS ALONG THE BANGANGA RIVER ,DISTRICT BHARATPUR, RAJASTHAN

Fig. 1

1. Santruk, Tehsil Bharatpur

The mound is located in the middle of the village on the right bank of the river. Most of it is occupied by modern structures; a small part measuring 400 x 400 x 8 m is free from modern habitation. The ceramics recovered from the mound are Painted Grey Ware (hereafter abbreviated PGW), plain grey ware, Kushan red ware sherds and a few medieval vases and *handis*. The grey ware sherds represent bowl and dish with black painted dots and wavy lines on the outer as well as the inner sides.

2. Rarh, Tehsil Bharatpur

The ancient mound of Rarh is located in the south-east of the village, 5 km away of Santruk. It has been disturbed and occupied by a late medieval mosque which is locally called Jami Masjid. The ceramics recovered from the mound are PGW, grey ware, Kushan red ware and medieval potsherds represented by bowl, dish, lid, jar and basin.

3. Awar, Tehsil Bharatpur

It lies on the Bharatpur-Mathura road, close to the Homes Canal on the right bank of the river. A *kachha* path leads to the mound from the metalled road. A disturbed mound is located in the centre of the village and measures 300 x 300 x 3 m. The ceramics recovered from the mound are PGW, black slipped ware, Kushan red ware and a few medieval potsherds.

4. Sogar, Tehsil Bharatpur

The village Sogar is located on the left bank of the river, 2 km away from Awar. The mound lies on the south-east of the village. It measures 800 x 800 m with a height of 5 m. The potteries from the sites consist of PGW, plain grey ware, Kushan red ware represented by dish, lid and bowl. The designs on PGW comprise criss-cross pattern and group of vertical strokes.

5. Dehra, Tehsil Bharatpur

It is located 3 km away from Borai on the right bank of the river. The mound lies close to the Homes Canal on the south-west and measures 800 x 800m with a height of 5 m. Most important of the pottery recovered from the site is PGW of fine fabric represented by bowl and dish. The site was once explored by the State Archaeological Department, Rajasthan; the reported N.B.P. was not found in the present exploration.

6. Methna, Tehsil Bharatpur

Methna lies on the Bharatpur-Kumher road. It is locally known Nagla Methna. It is 3 km away from Borai on the right bank of the Banganga. This small mound, measuring 50 x 50 m. is almost level with ground and covered with bushes. The ceramics recovered from the site are PGW and grey ware of fine to medium fabric. The fragments of bowl and dish, painted with black pigment depict wavy bands, vertical lines and dots. Absence of any other ceramics prove it to be a single culture site.

7. Bori, Tehsil Bharatpur

This village is located at about 8 km away from Bharatpur city, close to the Bharatpur-Dig road. The mound is situated in the centre of the village, partly occupied by habitation and measures 400 x 400 x 3 m. A few potsherds picked up from the site are PGW of fine fabric represented by bowl and dish, decorated with geometrical designs. The red ware sherds and structural remains of the Kushan period are also noticed at the site.

8. Bhandor, Tehsil Bharatpur

Bhandor, an important site lies on the Bharatpur-Mathura road. The site is located at the confluence of M.M. Canal with Homes Canal. The local legends ascribe this place to be the centre of *Dwaginimochan*. The site was earlier known as Bhandirvana, connected with Lord Krishna, who was believed to have saved the cows and cowherds from 'Evil Fire'. Bhandor is an extensive mound measuring 500 x 500 x 6m in east-west orientation. The exposed section of the mound to wards the west was scraped in proper way. The deposit is marked by the occurrence of PGW, associated by grey ware, black slipped ware and red ware. There is, however, no clear evidence of the presence of the Northern Black Polished ware but a few sherds of associated-red ware like the carinated *handi*, etc. were picked up. Kushan wares were found in profusion which are commonly found from most of the sites in Bharatpur, which being an adjoining territory of Mathura, the capital of the Kushanas is but natural. In addition, occurrence of Gupta pottery, being distinguished by its red slip and moulded designs, which are not so commonly found in other explored sites of Bharatpur, is notable.

9. Kasoda, Tehsil Bharatpur

The site is located close to the Bharatpur-Nadbai metre gauge railway line to the north of the present habitational area. The mound has been levelled for cultivation by the villagers. The circumference is about 800 m. The ceramics are PGW and plain grey ware of medium fabric along with coarse red wares.

10. Nagla Tuhiram, Tehsil Bharatpur

The village Nagla Tuhiram is about 10 km away from Bharatpur city on the Bharatpur-Sonkh road. The mound is located about 1 km away on the east of the village and measures 500 x 500 m with a height of 1.5 m. The site yielded Kushan, Rajput and medieval potsherds. The mound has been damaged and is capped by a late medieval temple. Fragments of pillars, and sculptures are found scattered on the site. The site belongs to the late medieval period.

11. Sewar, Tehsil Bharatpur

Sewar is a small town of the district Bharatpur on the Bharatpur—Jaipur National High Way. It was reported by the State Department of Archaeology, Rajasthan. This extensive mound, measuring 800 x 800 m with a height of about 10 m is located on the ancient Banganga river bed. The site has been damaged by modern structures. The finds are Ochre Colour Ware, black-and-red ware, PGW, grey ware, black slipped ware, Kushan red ware to early medieval potteries, similar to those of Noh.

12. Tatamar, Tehsil Bharatpur

This huge site is reported earlier by the State Department of Archaeology, Rajasthan. The measurement of the mound is about 600 x 600 x 8 m and is partly occupied by the villagers. The ceramics recovered from the mound are PGW and plain grey ware of fine fabric similar to those from Sewar. Dark red ware with black painting on the rim picked up from the site is identical with the typical Rang Mahal pottery of Rajasthan.

13. Bagdhari, Tehsil Bharatpur

It is 4 km away from Sewar on the Bharatpur-Jaipur road. A *kachha* path leads to the site from the metalled road. The mound measuring 400x400x8m lies on the north-west of the village. The ceramics recovered from the mound are PGW of fine to medium fabric, plain grey ware, black slipped ware, Kushan red ware and glazed ware of the medieval period. The site might have been deserted for a long time after the Kushanas because no finds of the Gupta and Rajput period is noticed during the survey.

14. Jheelra, Tehsil Bharatpur

Village Jheelra lies on the Ghana-Sewar metalled road, 6 km away from Bharatpur and nearer to Noh. The mound, measuring 600x400 m with a height of 1.5 m. from the ground level, is located on the west of the village, free from habitation. The potteries picked up from the site are similar to those from Noh except for the Ochre Coloured Ware. The black-and-red ware represented by bowl is of very fine fabric which has been reported from other nearby sites explored by the author. PGW, plain grey ware, black slipped ware, Kushan red ware and other historical ceramics including medieval coarse red were also picked up from the site. The site was most probably damaged from time to time by the floods of the Banganga river which was flowing very close to it in ancient times.

15. Par, Tehsil Bharatpur

Par is situated 1 km away from Bagdhari on Bharatpur-Jaipur road. The mound is small oval in shape, measuring 200x100x3 m. It has yielded red ware sherds represented by vase, bowl and lid of the Kushan period.

16. Bhaut, Tehsil Roopbas

The village Bhaut is located 26 km away from Roopbas on the Roopbas-Bharatpur road. The mound, situated in the centre of the village, measuring 800x 800x8m, is capped by modern structures and huge trees. The potteries picked up from the mound are red and black ware sherds represented by vase, jar, basin and lid of early medieval period.

17. Kharhera, Tehsil Roopbas

Kharhera lies on the Sewar-Uchhain road about 24 km away from Roopbas, close to the Uchhain Canal. The mound, measuring 50x50x3 is partly occupied and capped by *Neem* and *Chhokar* trees. The ceramics picked are red and coarse grey ware sherds of medieval times represented by vase, jar, lid and basin.

18. Uchain, Tehsil Roopbas

Uchain, a small town of Tehsil Roopbas lies and on Sewar-Bayana road. The mound measuring

800x800x10 m is located in the centre of the town and is partly capped by modern structures. The finds ar e red, black and coarse grey ware of m edieval period represented by jar, vase, basin and lid.

19. Andiyari, Tehsil Roopbas

Andiyari village lies on the Uchain-Bayana road. The mound is located across the Banganga river, measuring 300x300x5 m. The ceramics recovered from the surface belong to the medieval period, represented by the storage jar, basin, lid and a terracotta fragmentary spout.

20. Bachhamdi, Tehsil Nadbai

Bachhamdi lies on the Bharatpur-Bayana railway line. The ancient mound, measuring 100x100 m with a hight of 3 m, situated in the centre of village is partly occupied by habitation. The ceramics recovered from the mound belong to the medieval period represented by lid, vase, jar and basin of red ware. Fragmentary sculptures of medieval period depicting Vishnu and Siva have also been noticed on the surface of the mound.

21. Pingora, Tehsil Nadbai

Pingora is a small railway station which lies on the Bharatpur-Bayana railway line. The mound is located to the north-east of the village and measures 150x150x10m. It is partly occupied by the palaces of Jat rulers of Bharatpur. The finds from the site belong to the medieval period and consist of red, black and grey ware sherds represented by storage jar, basin and lid.

22. Pichuna, Tehsil Roopbas

Pichuna lies on the Bharatpur-Baseri road. The huge mound measuring 1000x1000 m with a height of 15 m is located close to the Pichuna Canal. The mound has been damaged by modern construction of a Government Secondary School on its top. The ceramics recovered from the surface of the mound are grey ware sherds of fine fabric which are generally found in association with PGW, tiny sherds of coarse black-and-red ware, black slipped ware and dark red ware sherds having painting on the rim resembling typical Rang Mahal ware. The important representative shape is the carinated *handi*. A few potsherds of medieval times including Chinese glazed ware are also noticed.

23. Bansi, Tehsil Wer

Bansi is a small village on the Bharatpur-Jaipur National Highway, close to the Banganga river bed. A *kachha* path leads to the site from Malena. The disturbed site with a little undisturbed por tion measuring 100x50 m with a height of 1m is to be seen in the centre of the village. The ceramics from the site are red ware sherds of medieval times representing jar, lid, *hindi* and basin.

24. Dharsnoi, Tehsil Wer

Dharsoni village lies on the Bharatpur-Jaipur road, close to the ancient Banganga river bed. Leaving a small part measuring 100x50x1m the major portion of the mound has been damaged by river flood. The ceramics from the mound are mainly red ware of Kushan times represented by bowl, dish including a few fragments of jar and basin of medieval times.

25. Rahimgarh, Tehsil Wer

Rahimgarh is 50 km away from Bharatpur on the Bharatpur-Jaipur National Highway. A *kachha* path towards the south along the Banganga basin leads to the village. The site is badly disturbed by floods leaving a little part measuring 300 300 m. intact. The ceramics recovered from the site are of the Kushan period while structural remains including buried ruins of Fort are of medieval times.

26. Halena, Tehsil Wer

Helena lies on the Bharatpur-Jaipur National Highway. The mound, in the north-west of the village is close to the Banganga river bed and has been eroded badly by floods. A few sherds picked up from the site are red ware of the Kushan period represented by bowl and lid.

27. Maloni, Tehsil Wer

Maloni is a small village on the Bharatpur-Jaipur road on the right side of Banganga river. The mound lies in the east of the village in totally washed out condition. The pottery picked up from the site is of medieval times.

28. Sarsena, Tehsil Wer

The village Sarsena lies on the right side of Banganga river. The mound measuring 600x600x8 m is located close to the Bharatpur-Jaipur National Highway. The ceramics from the site are fine grey ware, generally found in association with PGW, black slipped ware and Kushan red ware represented by bowl, dish and lid.

29. Netwari, Tehsil Wer

Netwari is located 10 km away on the south-west of Sarsena. The Banganga river has badly damaged the southern part of the mound. A few sherds belonging to the late medieval period were picked up from the rain gullies.

30. Bachhrain, Tehsil Wer

Bachhrain is 60 km away from Bharatpur on the Bharatpur-Jaipur National Highway, close to the Banganga river bed. The extensive mound measuring 1000x800x3 m has been disturbed from time to time by the floods of the Banaganga river. The potteries recovered from the site reveal the cultural assemblage right from the protohistoric period to the historical period. The ceramics found are : plain black-and-red ware, PGW and grey ware of fine fabric black slipped ware and the Kushan red ware.

Observation

The present exploration throws ample light on the sites of archaeological importance right from protohistoric times to late the medieval period.

There is a greater concentration of black-and-red ware, black slipped ware and PGW in the area between Santruk and Jheelra i.e. the upper or eastern Banganga. The black-and-red ware found in this area is quite different from that of Ahar. In 1963-64 when Noh was excavated the black-and-red ware with a separate phase has been recognised as a preceding culture of the PG Ware in the contiguous area of eastern Rajasthan. On the basis of this and keeping in view the sequence of Noh, it may be postulated that there could have been pre-PGW phase in this region. It appears that the extension of this culture is not well-marked in the south-westerly direction for about 60 km along the Banganga river bed from Unchagaon to Malkhera. It may be due to the arid condition that had set in or one to some natural calamities as the only source of water in this area was the rains. The area around Bharatpur has brakish sub-soil water. The geophysical survey carried out by L. N. Kailasam and party in 1949-50 found patches of land where ground water level was highly saline. The proto-historic people were accustomed to live in the open and fertile land along the banks of the river which could not be found by them in the south-westerly area of district Bharatpur. The eastern part of the district was fertile plain where protohistoric sites are located at a distance of 3 to 5 km from each other.

It has, however, to be added that the deluxe ware, Northern Black polished is conspicuous by its absence, though its associated wares are found along the Banganga river bed. Excavation at Noh also revealed Northern Black Polished ware in limited quantity. It may be presumed that by about 5th and 3rd century B.C. this area was deserted or was affected by salinity or arid climate which should have affected economic status of potters so that the use of this deluxe ware declined.

Once again this valley has undergone rejuvenation during the early centuries of Christian era which yielded a large number of red ware of the Kushan as well as later periods along the lower Banganga. Only few sites yielded Rang Mahal type of pottery which seems not to be of the local culture.

Select Bibliography

1. Ghosh, A. The Rajputana desert : its archaelogical aspect, Proceeding of symposium on Rajputana desert. *Bulletin of the National Institute of Science of India*, New Delhi 1952 pp. 37-42.
2. Gupta, S.P. Painted Grey Ware Sites in relation to old river beds in Rajasthan in Agarwal, D.P. and Pande, B.M. (ed.) *Ecology and Archaeology in western India* New Delhi 1977, pp. 89-92.
3. Negi, B.S. Distribution of Painted Grey Ware Sites in district Bharatpur, Rajasthan, *Puratattva*, No. 12, New Delhi, pp. 129-132.
4. Indian Archaeology 1963-64—A Review, pp. 28-29.
   ,, 1965-66—A Review, p. 38.
   ,, 1966-67—A Review. p. 30.
   ,, 1977-78—A Review. p. 46.
   ,, 1978-79 – A Review. p. 19.
   ,, 1984-85—A Review (In Press).
5. Rao, M.B.R. and Negi, B.S. Geophysical Exploration in the Arid Tracts of Rajaputana, Proceeding of Symposium on Rajputana desert. *Bulletin of the National Institute of Science of India*, New Delhi 1952. pp. 70-75.
6. Singh R.L. *India A Regional Geography*, National Geographical Society of India, Varanasi 1971, p. 524.

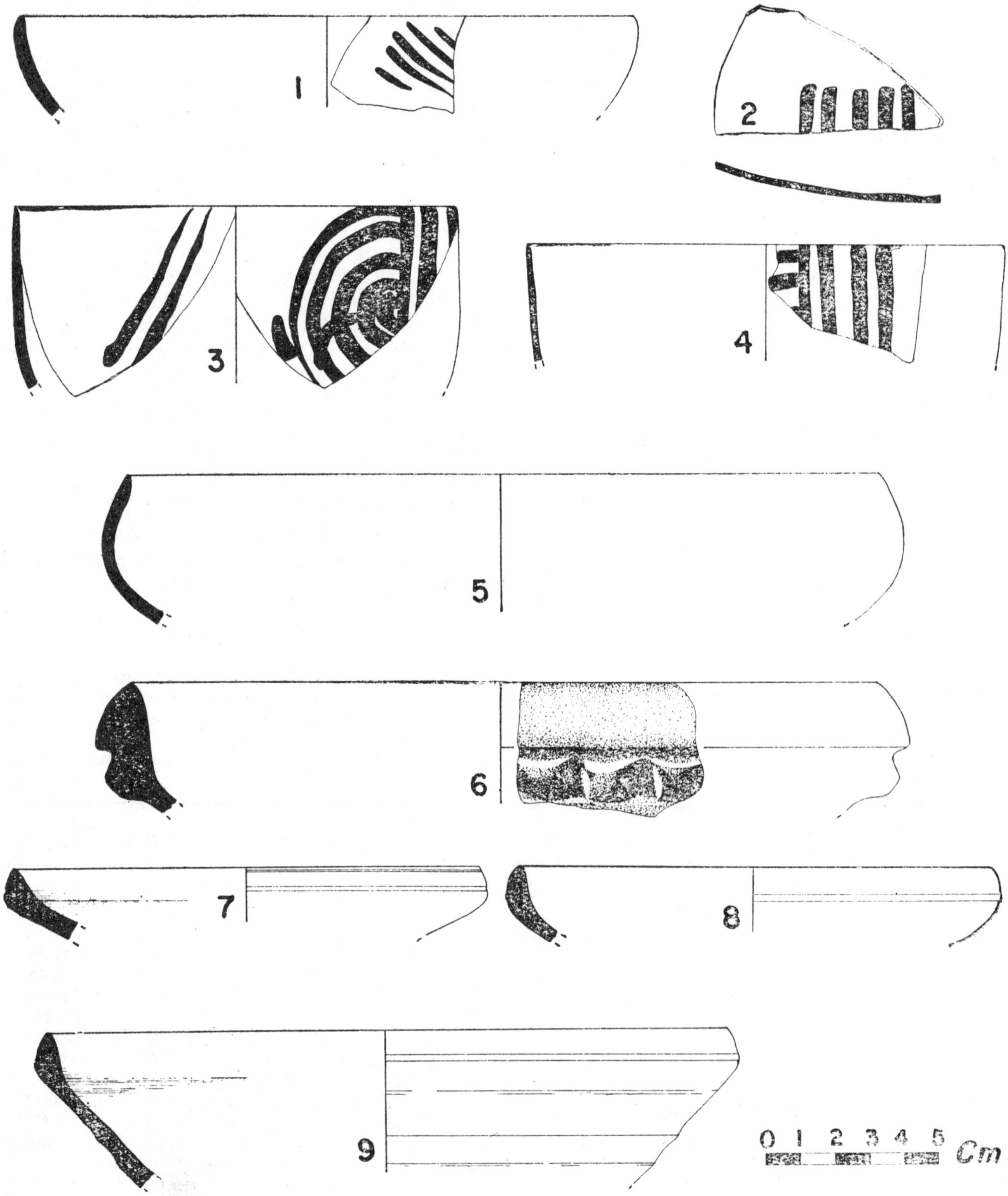

Fig. 2. Bhandor : 1-4, PGW ; 5, Grey ware ; 6-9, Red ware.

3

Painted Grey Ware Culture in Garhwal, Himalaya : New Evidence and Interpretation

K. P. Nautiyal, B.M. Khanduri, Vinod Nautiyal, D. L. Rajput and R. K. Bhatt

Archaeological investigations in Garhwal, Himalaya till 1975 were mainly discoveries of inscriptions and temples. Scholars were inclined to believe that the whole of the central Himalaya did not witness the rise and growth of the protohistoric cultures. Nevertheless, on account of an active field work—exploration and excavation—the chronological framework of Garhwal has not only been pushed back but several new aspects, particularly of the presence of Painted Grey Ware culture, in this part of Himalaya has been established. The discovery of Painted Grey Ware culture at Thapli (Alkananda valley) and Purola (Yamuna valley) has now firmly established the advent and growth of this culture in the Himalayan region.

The Painted Grey Ware culture found in a greater part of the sub-continent from Bahawalpur[1] in the north-west in Pakistan to Punjab and Haryana in the north-east extends further to a major part of the Ganga-Yamuna *Doab.* The concentration of this culture is noticed in Punjab, Haryana, north-eastern Rajasthan and the upper Ganga-Yamuna basin in U.P. In the west the P.G.W. has also been reported from Lakhiyo Pir in Sind. The easternmost site of the PGW is Sravasti in U.P.[2] Towards southwards it is towards as far as Ujjain[3] with such sites in between as Akoda, Barata[4] in Bhind and further ahead at Kutwar[5] on the bank of Asan in Morena district of M.P., thus stretching the main Painted Grey Ware area from the Ganga-Yamuna *doab* further south.

So far as the northernmost limit of the Ganga-Yamuna *doab* is concerned, evidences of the discovery of PGW have come forth from places like Ahichchhatra,[6] Bijnor and Saharanpur,[7] which are roughly between two hundred to two hundred-fifty kilometres from the Himalayan region of Garhwal. In the past it was believed that the PGW people did not penetrate mountain region[8] and confined themselves to the Indo-Gangetic plains. However, a new discovery of this ware from Garhwal takes the PGW right into the interiors of the Himalayas extending the boundary to the extreme mid-north India.

The first site of PGW falling in Tehri Garhwal is Thapli[9] (30° 12′ N, 78° 47′ E). Located on the right bank of river Alakananda, just on the other flank of Srinagar town, the site has already been disturbed by a massive road-cutting. The total thickness of the deposit is 2.90 m, out of which 1.70 m has totally vanished in road-cutting operation. To begin with, a trial trench was laid out directly on the road surface measuring 5 x 2 m. Digging vertically to assess the thickness of the occupational deposit, the excavation revealed a single phase culture of PGW along with its associaled wares and their associated types.

This habitational deposit at Thapli-1 (TPL-1) consisted of three layers with a total thickness of 1.20 m resting on a well-laid out river pebbles mixed with natural soil, yellow and sticky in nature.

The shapes in PGW from this site is confined mainly to dish and bowl. However, a miniature vase with painting is quite interesting. The type has earlier been reported from Ahichchhatra,[10] Noh[11] and Atranjikhera.[12] The vase may be associated with some ritual as has been proposed by Sinha in regard to the miniature vases found in the red ware from Sravasti.[13] The discovery of such a miniature vase with paintings from PGW levels appears to have carried an early association with the late Harappan shape as propounded by

Joshi from his evidence of this type of a grey vase discovered at Bhagwanpura.[14]

The Thapli PGW has several painted designs, such as the sun symbol along with horizontal and vertical bands, horizontal rim bands, dots, sigmas, concentric circles, intersecting strokes, wavy lines, spirals, double lines with dots, leaf, floral patterns, etc. showing in most of the cases a maturity in the art of painting. A notable point to mention is that both the thin and thick varities of this ware are available here with paintings (Pl. 1).

The associated pottery from Thapli consists of black slipped, fine red, grey and coarse red wares. But the frequency of the PGW is roughly 10 per cent of the total pottery. The main shapes in the associated wares are dishes, bowls, vases and basins. It is interesting to note that some shapes like the basins and the vases are found both in the coarse red ware as well as in the plain grey ware. In one case in the red ware a vase is perforated. It is pertinent to add here that perforated vessels are reported from Hastinapura, Atranjikhera, Ahichchhatra, Sravasti, Ropar, Sardargarh, Chak and Allahpur; all PGW sites in northern India. The red ware from Thapli also contains incised decoration.

Among other finds is a perfectly baked pale red terracotta bird, decorated with notches on the body (Pl. 2). A similar bird in PGW fabric with an incised cross pattern at the back and pierced dots for eyes is also reported from Noh.[15] The finds from Thapli included copper bangles, copper nail parers and terracotta beads along with one *ghata*-shaped bead. A few coarse red ware sherds depicting husk marks indicate paddy cultivation and use of rice as a staple diet.

The analysis of faunal remains from Thapli has brought to light dental and osteological remains of the domesticated animals of *Bos indicus* (Indian humped cattle), *Sus Scrofa Cristatus* (domestic pig) and *Equus cabalus*—domestic horse[16]—(Pl. 3). On the basis of identation and fracture marks on limb bones and jaws, it has been suggested that the inhabitants of Thapli butchered adult and matured animals for their food. A similarity can be drawn with the animal remains from Hastinapura.[17] This suggests that the PGW inhabitants in all parts of the country had fascination for a particular type of cattle for their dietary needs.

Another important site of PGW in Garhwal was discovered at Purola (31⁰ 70′ N. 78⁰ 40′ E),[18] which is situated on the left bank of river Kamal, a tributary of the Yamuna in the Uttarkashi district. The site is not well preserved due to later disturbances.

Two vertical trenches (PRL-3 and PRL-4) were laid near the road surface having a dimension of 5 x 3 m. The excavation revealed a single phase culture of PGW along with its associated material. The habitational deposit at Purola-3 (PRL-3) and Purola-4 (PRL-4) consisted of three layers with a total thickness of 1.10 m resting on a weathered a sandstone rock.

The PGW from this site is confined mainly to the dish and bowl types. The paintings on this ware are restricted to horizontal and vertical bands, concentric circles and dots. The associated pottery from Purola consists of red slipped, black slipped, grey and red wares. The main shapes in the associated wares are dishes, bowls and vases (Pl 4).

Among the other finds terracotta lion, disc, cone, ball, hopscotch, bead (*ghata*-shaped) and potter's stamp are worth mentioning.

The animal remains from Purola show dental and femur remains of *Equus cabalus* (domestic horse). It is worth mentioning that horse bones have been found in the excavations of the PGW sites in India.

Since the discovery of Painted Grey ware in Garhwal is significant, it would be worthwhile to discuss and correlate the literary evidences pertaining to the region with the available archaeological data. In case the PGW is taken to be associated with some branch of the Aryan group or with the Mahabharata story as suggested by Lal,[19] Garhwal provides ample testimony in the great epic and other Puranic literature that the region was very much known to the people of ancient Aryavarta. The holiness of the rivers Ganga (Alkananda and Bhagirathi) and Yamuna has been greatly extolled on account of the *Tirtha-yatra* (religious pilgrimage) as also episode of the Gangavataran—descent of river Ganga—which rises in the Himalaya. In the Mahabharata, in the context of the visit of Panchal (the region of Ahichchhatra) by the Pandavas and the defeat of Gandharva Chitraratha by Arjuna we find a description of Alkananda as a most holy river, which descends from the Himalaya along with seven other rivers.[20] Similarly at other place the poet has explicitly described the geographical situation of the two rivers—Alkananda and Bhagirathi—which meet at a point and are jointly designated as Ganga.[21] In one more reference in the Aryanakaparva, Krishna is stated to have propitiated sage Narayana on Mount Gandhamadana and later conducted a very complicated penance at Badrikashrama.[22] In the *Mahaprasthanika parva*[23] of the Mahabharata a vivid description of the Himalayan land of Garhwal is significant. It is to be mentioned here that after coming to know about the great havoc of war, the five Pandava brothers, along with Draupadi undertook a *prithvipradakshina* or circumambulation of the earth. After completion of the four rounds of the earth they proceed for *svargarohana*. In this context (*Svargarohana*), the description of the Brahma river, Pancha Prayag and Kedar is important. The mention of Pancha Prayagas is significant and can be rightly associated with the existing five important pilgrim centres of Garhwal, viz. Devaprayag, Rudra Prayag, Karna Prayag, Nanda Prayag and Vishnu Prayag, almost all located on way to Badrinath.

This testimony in the Mahabharata is further supplemented by the other vedic and puranic records, which tell something about the Khasas[24] who are supposed to have lived in this area along with other tribes. The Khasas were taken by an earlier study to be a branch of the Aryan stock. Khasas and Kiratas[25] were dwelling around the sources of the Ganga and Yamuna. Thus such descriptions in various literary texts do present a similar picture suggesting that the PGW people did migrate and lived in the Himalayan region of Garhwal, particularly along the banks of Alkananda, Bhagirathi and the Yamuna.

Taking into consideration all historical and literary aspects of Garhwal Himalaya, Tucci's[26] views seem to be relevent and also make us think about the constantly migrating hordes of tribes in this part of the central Himalayan region in about the second millennium B.C. The great process of migration appears to have continued here for a pretty long time, say up to the beginning of the first millennium B.C. As mentioned earlier, the Puranic geographical description also gives explicit account of all the tribes together in a group suggesting that they lived in the Himalaya, probably under some confederation as suggested by Tucci.[27] The Puranas and the Mahabharata together mention the names of some tribal groups like the Khasas, Kiratas, Rajya Kiratas and Nagas, who were flourishing in this part of the Himalaya. These homogeneous group of tribes settled themselves widely in this part of the country after covering a long course of migration from their ancestral homeland.

In the light of the above, we are inclined to believe that the PGW culture was undoubtedly associated with a process of migration of various communities to a major part of central and western Himalaya. The dispersal of PGW in the Himalayas was through the two sacred rivers—the Ganga and the Yamuna. Himalaya probably witnessed the first efflorscence of the Painted Grey Ware culture presumably on account of the cultural cross-currents from the Indo-Gangetic plains or from the north-western part of the country which became a focal point of all the migrating hordes during the second—first millennium B.C.

References

1. Mughal, M.R. New Archaeological evidence from Bahawalpur, *Man and Environment*, Vol. IV, pp. 93-98.
2. Sinha, K.K. *Excavations at Sravasti—1959*, Varanasi 1967.
3. Banerji, N.R. *Indian Archaeology—A Review 1956-57*, p. 20.
4. *Indian Archaeology—A Review 1958-59*, p. 26.
5. Nautiyal, K.P. Cultural Interaction in North-Western Madhya Pradesh and the Role of Rivers during the First Millenium B.C.: An Assessment, *Archaeological Congress and Seminar : 1972*, Singh, U.V. (ed.). Kurukshetra University, Kurukshetra, 1976.
6. Panigrahi, K.C. and Ghosh, A. The pottery of Ahichchhatra, *Ancient India*, No. 1, pp. 36-59.
7. Deshpande, M.N. Painted Grey Ware in Ganga Valley, *Seminar on the Painted Grey Ware*, Aligarh (in press) and also in *Indian Archaeology—A Review 1963* to *1969*.
8. Tripathi, Vibha. *The Painted Grey Ware—An Iron Age Culture of Northern India*, 1976, p. 8.
9. Nautiyal, K.P., Khanduri, B.M., Nautiyal, Vinod and Rajput, Thapli, D.L. A Painted Grey Ware site in Garhwal, *Puratattva*, No. 10, pp. 94-95.
10. Panigrahi and Ghosh, 1945. *op. cit*, pp. 36-59.
11. *Indian Archaeology —A Review 1962-64*, pp. 28-29.
12. Gaur, R.C. Painted Grey Ware at Atrahjikhera—An Assessement in B.P. Sinha (ed.). *Potteries in Ancient India*, 1969, pp. 113-114.
13. Sinha 1967. *op. cit*.
14. Joshi, J.P. A Note on Excavation at Bhagwanpura, *Puratattva* No. 8, p. 180.
15. *Indian Archaeology—A Review 1962-64*, pp. 28-29; *1968-69* and *1970-71*.

16. Badam. G.L. Faunal remains from Thapli, a PGW site near Srinagar, U.P.—a preliminary report, *Thapli excavation Report* (in Press).

17. Nath, Bhola in Lal, B.B. Excavation of the Hastinapura and other exploration in the upper Ganga and Sutlej Basin 1950-52, New light on the Dark Age between the End of the Harappan culture and the Early Historical period, *Ancient India,* No. 10-11, pp. 107-120.

18. The ancient site of Purola was excavated by the Department in 1986-87 under the direction of Prof. K.P. Nautiyal with assistance from B.M. Khanduri, Dr. Vinod Nautiyal, Dr. D.L. Rajput, Sarvashri V.P. Hatwal, R.K. Bhatt, Pradeep Saklani and Govind Nautiyal. Technical help was provided by Sarvashri J.S. Rawat and J.S. Negi.

19. *Ancient India,* 10 & 11, p. 151.

20. *Mahabharata, Adiparva,* ch. 158, verse 15-21.

21. *Ibid.*

22. *Ibid., Aryanka-parva,* ch. 13, verse 10-13.

23. Belvalkar, S.K. *The Mahaprasthanika Parvan,* Vol. 19, T.S.M.-10. 5, Poona, 1959.

24. Nautiyal, K.P. *The Archaeology of Kumaun,* 1969, pp. 17-20

25. *Ibid.*, p. 15

26. Tucci, G. On Swat, The Dards and Connected Problems. *East and West,* Vol. 27, p. 35

27. *Ibid.*, p. 36

4

New Light on Vengipura: Excavations at the Ancient Historical City of Andhradesa

I. K. Sarma

Ancient Vengi, now a sprawling village called Peddavegi, 12 km north of Eluru town in district West Godavari (Lat 16°48′N Long 81°07′E) was a renowned capital city of the early ynasties like Salankayana, Vishnukundin and Chalukyan that ruled Andhradesa[1] from the middle of fourth to eleventh century A.D. The Salankayanas and *Salankayanka* i.e. the country of the Salankayanas, were first mentioned by Panini[2] (6th century B.C.). It is certain that *Salakenoi* governed from Vengi as early as A.D. 140 as attested by Ptolemy[3] who mentioned the place along with other important port towns such as *Maisolos* (Machilipatnam), Koddura or Kuduru (Guduru) and Kantakossyla (Ghantasala), on the eastern seaboard (Fig. 1). All

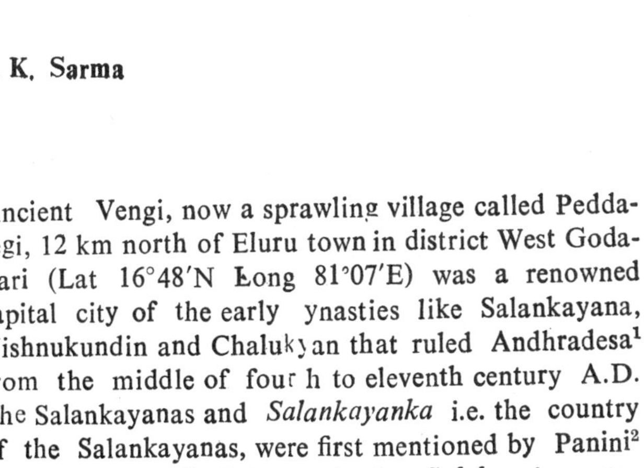

Fig. 1. Location of Peddavegi

these places were strongholds of Buddhism and humming with merchants from eastern[4] as well as western countries. According to a newly discovered inscription on a sculptured pillar part, we learn about one Salankayana minister named Bhutila stationed[5] at Kausambi (U.P.). Samudragupta, the Imperial Gupta King, mentions *Vaingeyaka* Hastivarman (I), among the rulers subjugated by him in the Andhra country.[6] Salankayanas rose to power immediately after the fall of the later Satavahana and Ikshvaku dynasties and made Vengi, their seat (*adhisthana*). Hiuen Tsang (A.D. 639-40), the Chinese pilgrim refers to *Ping-ki-Polo* (Vengipura) as the capital city in *Antolo* and speaks of a *Stupa* built by Asoka Maurya at this place.[7]

Robert Sewell was the first to visit the place in 1888 when the ancient mound of Dhanamdibba, north of the village was being dug out by the locals.[8] He noted that "the centre of this mound had not been dealt, and if, as appears, this is a *Stupa*, the relic casket may still be there". Alexander Rea (1902) listed several ancient places here for protection.[9] During the years 1985-87 the Excavation Branch (I) Nagpur, under the direction of the author has undertaken in a phased manner, digging at three places, (1) PVG-I-*Dhanam dibba* site literally "mound of wealth", (2) PVG-II-the Paramesvara Temple and (3) PVG-III-west of the village across the fortifications.

Three phases of cultural activity, all assignable to the early historical period, were brought to light. The occupation being continuous, dating of the three phases was based on the associated structural, sculptural, numismatic and cult objects. Thus Phase-IA was that of the Salankayana times, *circa* 4th to 5th century A.D.; Phase-IB, Vishnukundin, mid-5th to end of 6th century A.D., and Phase-IC, Eastern Chalukyan, end of 6th and early 7th century A.D.

A. Stupa at Dhanamdibba (Figs. 2 and 3)

A massive structural complex of brick was exposed in the centre of the mound PVG-I, which is identified as a *Stupa* with an entrance porch towards east. The unit consists of a solidly built brick *Stupa* at the centre (Pl. 1) over a square platform measuring 12.90 m and preserved to a height of 1.75 m. The basal plan at the dome part is squarish on plan and measures 10.70 m. It resembles the *Chaitya* of Ghantasala in its central layout of bricks in a stepped pattern; the bottom most cube being 3.06 m. An inner circumambulatory passage 45 cm wide was provided around the dome, whereas the outer *pradakshinapatha* was of 2.40 m wide around the drum which measured 12.90 m square, and preserved to a height of 1.75 metres only. The dome exterior appears to have been originally encased with sculptured limestone slabs and stucco work which according to Robert Sewell were removed by locals, but the drum appears to be plain. The extant height of the dome works out to be 1.20 m while its diameter is 10.70 m. Originally, it may have risen to a height of 13 m.

At the four corners of the *prakara* rectangular chambers or platforms 2.70x2.25m were built in phase IB. These chambers appear to take the place of *ayakas*, a characteristic feature of the Andhra *Stupas*. Further the *Stupa*-complex has an elaborate

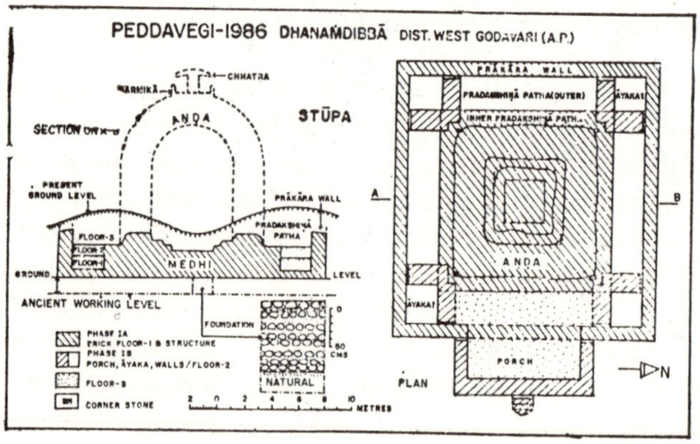

Fig. 2.

entrance porch at the east measuring 8.30×4.5 m with stepped *sopana* and moonstone descent marking the threshhold. In its central layout the Peddavegi *Stupa* resembles the *mahastupa* of Ghantasala, Dist. Krishna, excavated by Alexander Rea. A four line inscription in Brahmi characters of 4th century A.D. on an octagonal *mandapa* pillar infact refers to a person hailing from Ghantasala aligned to the *aparasaila* sect, who perhaps caused the *mandapa* pillar to be erected. The lotus medallions on the pillar sections and the characters of the record clearly suggest a post-Ikshvaku date to the monastic order of Peddavegi.[11] In fitness of things the *Stupa* here, like the one at Ghantasala, belongs to *Aparamaha Vinaseliyas*, a dominant sect based at *Sriparvata* (Nagarjunakonda). Basing on the earlier notices of Sewell, further digging was planned to record the foundational pattern and to ascertain if any relic is placed at the centre. Systematic removal of the brick courses was undertaken. In all twenty-six brick courses were carefully removed at the central part of the structure right upto its base. It was found that the earliest brick work was laid on a raised platform of 1.18m high comprising eight layers of river sand, rolled stone and silt packed in perfect horizontal bands. This foundation was limited to the *medhi* (drum) part only because of the superload whereas at the outside, the enclosure wall and *pradakshina* floors in between, were freely built over a levelled ground.

The associated finds include, apart from pottery wares, a meagre quantity of decoratives like stucco flowers, a limestone plaque depicting *Srivatsa*, a Nandi in a bas-relief panel and human face, beads and ear-ornaments, etc. The *Stupa*-complex appears to be the work of the Salankayana ruler, possibly Nandivarman-II (A.D. 400-430), who according to a pillar inscription from the nearby Guntupalle[12] caves (27 km north of Peddavegi) is reported to have caused certain major donations to the Buddhist *viharas* while ruling from the victorious city of Peddavegi in spite of his being a *Paramabhagavata* and devoted to *Chitraratha Svami*.

B. Panchayatana-Complex Phase-1B (Pl. 2)

Trenches were laid north of the above *Stupa*-complex. They revealed an extensive brick structure, rectangular on plan and measuring 19.40 x 176.0 m

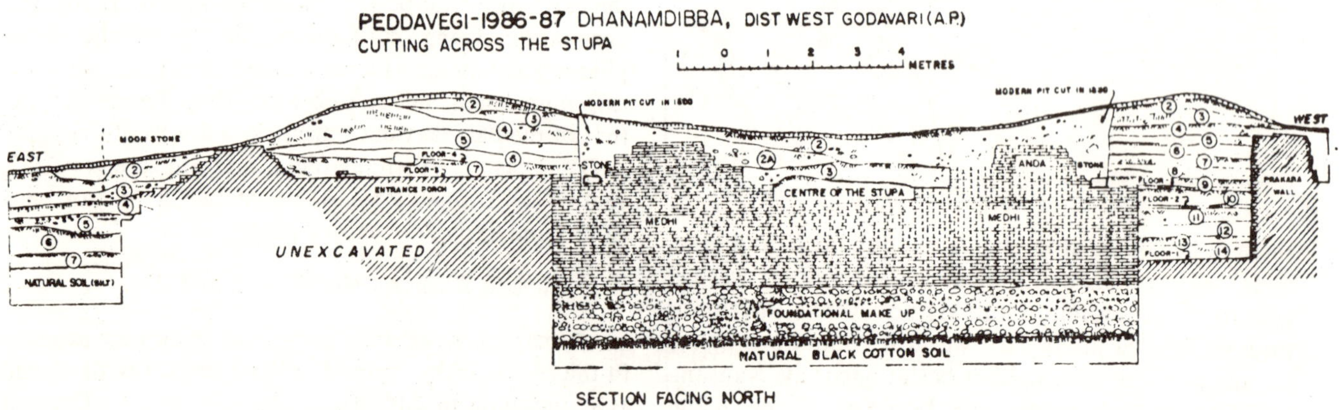

Fig. 3.

with the main entrance eastwards. The common *adhisthana* has an impressive *jagati* and *tripatta kumuda*, out of cut and chamfered bricks, to a height of 0.75 m. The *kumuda* is bound by *urdhva* and *adhah padma* decor and plastered uniformly to impart a *padmadala* look. The bricks are of the size of 42x21x8 or 37x 18x7.5 cm with a fine joinery. The side wall is extant to a height of 1.6 m but this height was not achieved in one phase but is the result of two distinct phases of structural activity. The topmost (Phase IC), wall is a jerry-built one above the *padavedi* of phase IB. This upper phase coincides with the addition of limestone *pranalas* at the southern side of the two (south-west and south-east) shrines.

The south side of the *panchayatana* is better preserved to a height of 2.35 m than its northern counterpart. Niches are seen at regular intervals enhancing the elevational grandeur. These niches possessed *kudya stambhikas* of circular form made of neatly chamfered bricks. They seem to be empty sham niches but the *bhitti* was well plastered and finished.

The niches at the northern face are heavily damaged but measured 1.40 m wide and like the southern face regularly spaced. In the western side they are of 98 cm wide and at irregular intervals. While at the eastern face they are of 60 cm. wide and flanked the main entrance; two on either side of the balustraded descents. On the basis of the layout and elevation of the structure, the number and placement of the wall niches (*bhadra koshthas*) the complex appears to possess four shrines at the four corners while at the centre a stepped well with a shrine was present. The shrines are approximately identical in size, and rectangular in shape. The central part was found very much damaged by the brick robbers. None of the shrines yielded any image and we are not certain of the associated religious cult to which this *panchayatana* can be exactly assigned. The addition of stone *pranalas* to two shrines at the south indicate the observance of *abhisheka* ritual. Deep digging at the Trench YA I Qdt.3, the earliest phase of this *panchayatana*-complex was found to be coevel with the phase of the *Stupa*. The brick *prakara* wall at the northern side of the *stupa* was infact given a facing of dressed sandstone blocks externally all through. This was apparently caused to protect the the wall as a drain was provided along the outer periphery of paved brick floor of the *panchayatana* which served as a *pradakshinapatha* to a width of nearly 2 m on all sides.

C. PVG-II: Paramesvara Temple Area

At the southern and eastern precincts of this temple, excavation was undertaken to ascertain the cultural sequence. Remains of two brick temples were traced (Pl. 3) below the stone temple of Paramesvara. These brick temple units, three in all, face west and on plan possess a square *garbhagriha*, an *antarala* and a *mandapa* in front. Around each unit was a *pradakshina* of 1.20 m wide. Post-holes in the shrine wall indicate a thatch roof on wooden posts above the wall. These brick shrines are of Vishnukundin period while the Paramesvara temple is of later Chalukyan date (10th century A.D.). In the upper levels, apart from the disturbed stone sub-plinth of Paramesvara temple, floral as well as figure parts of stucco work over the exterior of the stone wall were recovered.

D. PVG-III: Fortifications

A detailed surface examination and study of the ancient vestiges at this place revealed extensive ruins, including a fortified township encampassing the nearby hamlets to an extent of approximately 6 sq. km. Several ancient spots and mounds were dug out by the locals and deep pits within the village habitations and outside stand witness to the destruction of this famed city.

The gravel fortifications called *Kotadibbalu* encircle an area of one square km. These walls have been largely levelled up except at the west and partly southern extents. Identical images of Kalabhairava were found at the north-east and northern boundaries of the fortifications. Though disturbed from their *in situ* positions, these are valuable examples revealing the cult during the early Chalukyan times. The images are nude, two-handed with *khadga and churika* in both the hands and with *sarpalankaras*. They served as the guardian dieties (*Kshetranampatayah*) of the city of Vengipura in the same way as the ancient city of Varanasi.

Excavation across the Fortification

A vertical trench across the gravel fortifications extant at the western part was undertaken. The gravel make up of the fortification wall was to a thickness of 7.10 m above the first working level in distinct stages. A levelled ground was noted at a depth of 2.35 m marked by burnt hearth over a mud floor. Apart from pottery of Red Polished Ware, a miniature *linga* of limestone and an ivory pendent were found on this floor level. It appears that the workmen at the fortifications temporarily camped at the spot. A brick veneer is also found at this level along the western edge of the bund. Trial trenches were sunk at either ends of the gravel bund. A moat with silt and water-borne layers was traced at the western extent of the fortifications. Brick alignments indicating postern gateways were traced on the surface of the north-west and southern parts of the fortifications. The brick size and the pottery wares clearly indicate that the fortifications were caused during the Salankayana period and continued to be in use and perhaps strengthened during the subsequent phases.

II. Important finds

Among the objects recovered from the digs are two limestone pillar parts, one from Trench YA-1, Qdt. 3 and another from Trench ZA-1, Qdts. 3 and 4. Both measured 1.52 m in length and found along with the disturbed brick courses seemingly fallen from the wall along with the collapse of the structure.

(1). Inscribed pranalas (Pl. 4 a-c)

They are originally sculptured pillars of limestone with mid-octagonal sections marked with lotus medallions and running animal frieze at the terminals. Such pillars originally belong to a Buddhist *mandapa* but reused here as water-chutes (*pranalas*) by cutting a channel along the shorter sections moulded to resemble an elephant's trunk (*Gaja sundas*).

Both the *pranalas* revealed on their broader sections Brahmi inscriptions in 2nd century A.D. characters.[13] The first one from Tr. YA-1, Qdt. 3 has only two letters, reading *Daksha* standing perhaps for the name of a carver. The second example is far more important as it revealed two records on both its wider faces. We come to know for the first time a king named Kakichi (*Rajno Kakichikaya maha rajasa*) and cites certain monks and nuns connected to Maha-Nagaparvata i.e. the hill monastery of Guntupalle which is 27 km north of Peddavegi. In the second record this very king is stated to be a monk internee (*antevasaka*) at the Buddhist *sangha* of the place. It might be noted that no Buddhist structure assignable to second century A.D. was found at Peddavegi and the *Stupa* exposed at Dhanamdibba cannot be pushed to a date earlier than mid-4th century A.D. The Asokan *Stupa* referred to by Hieun Tsang has not been located anywhere among the Peddavegi ruins. The above inscriptions and the sculptured pillars no doubt push back the antiquity of Buddhism to early centuries A.D. However, the associated structures where in these sculptured pillars were reused as water-chutes belong to Phase-IC beginning, dated to the end of 6th and seventh century A.D. Who was this king named Kakichi? Is he any way connected to the toponym Kakinada? Do we have in him the origin for the later dynastic name Kakati? Was the name ending *Kaka* or *Kaki* denote the daughter as in Janaki from Janaka? All these are interesting to wit.

2. A Carnelian intaglio (Pl. 5b.)

Assignable to Phase-IA is a unique find of an intaglio measuring 2 x 2.6 cm,[14] ovalish in shape and 4.4 mm thick. This appears to be Royal seal. This precious object was found at the south-west entrance of a cut-stone veneered building within the inner city wall. A circular or elliptical shrine was partly exposed at this spot and during clearance operations (PVG 1984-85) this rare object was picked up. Plano-convex in section, over its reddish broad facet is a female beauty carved centrally in linear form, the skill, tools and techniques employed are beyond the pale of scientific analysis. The female standing in *abhanga*, facing front is two-handed, the right arm is half-raised holds a four-petalled lily (*nilotpala*), with the first finger and thumb. The left hand is at the upper part of the hip (*katisamsthita-hasta*). She has a bejewelled turreted crown over the head. The elongate neck, shapely shoulders strong at the root, sumptuous breasts, slender waist and prominent navel enhance her beautiful stance She has wide eyes, sharp nose and bulbous cheeks but shapely chin and prominent pout. The most interesting aspect lies in her apparel. The upper silken frock is largely transparent and ends with gems and pearls (*muktas*), entwined at the terminals. The lower *langa* or trouser like loose robe made of diaphanous silks has ornamented lace border whose ends are rolled up. The dress and turreted crown recall to mind the female deities depicted on Indo-Scythian or Kushan coins and seals dated to first century B.C. from North-West India.[15] The *kanthikas* in the neck and the *chakra kundala* in the right and the *makara* or *pushpa kundalas* in the left ear the *bhujakirtis* and wristlets and the slender body closely resembles the female forms on the relief sculptures of Amaravati and Nagarjunakonda. On the basis of the striking Hellenistic features of the head-dress and attire, the divine form on the intaglio like the *Kapisa* or *Pushkalavatinagara devatas*, can be regarded as a city goddess of Vengipura, serving both as the protectress of the city (*Durga* or *Amba*) as well as the *Rajyalakshmi* of the Salankayanas of Vengi. It may not be unreasonable to think that this was a legacy from the Gandhara country to south-east India by the royal house of the Salankayanas who migrated from North West and rose to power at Vengi.

3. Other antiquities

An assortment of limestone plaques with divinities

sculptured in bas-relief were found from Phase-IA and also early levels of IB. They reveal the existence of popular cults which worship of Siva-Sakti, Ganesa, Nagini and so on as pet Gods (*Ishtadevata*). These stone plaques in particular, betray the Ikshvaku art style though smaller in size. They mark the reemergence of Vedic and Brahmanical cults with Gods in human and symbolic forms during the later half of fourth and early 5th century A.D.

Siva-Parvati (Pl. 5a)

A limestone plaque (12x9 and 2.1 cm thick) showed a seated figure of Siva and Parvati carved in relief. Siva here has the third eye vertically shown between the eyebrows and is seated at ease along with Parvati on a *Manchaka adhishthana*. This is the earliest art object depicting Siva-Parvati in human form in south India and clearly anterior to the early Pallava *Somaskanda* reliefs. The symbolic-anthropomorphic plaques obtained from Madugula, Kunidene[17] (Guntur district), and Peddamudiyam (Cuddapah district), are later examples in this series.

Pancha Linga (Pl. 6c)

A grey sandstone plaque measuring and 2.5 cm 7x5x7 thick depicted in deep relief fine *lingas* in a row over a *padmapitha*, emphasising the symbolic aspect of Rudra as *Panchanana* or *Saranana*. This might also stand for *Panchavaktra* Siva. The plaque was undoubtedly an object of worship of a *Vaidika* of Vengipura.

Srivatsa-Sri and Sakti (Pl. 6b)

Other limestone objects recovered from the digs as well as from surface include a *Srivatsa Sri* with *Sakti* or spearhead. This example retains the characteristic features of the *Srivatsa* from depicted on the early Satavahana coins and art object of *circa* 2nd century B.C. date.

Mahishamardini (Pl. 6a)

A plaque depicting Mahishamardini in relief is another outstanding cult object from Peddavegi. The figure and the depiction closely recalls the 'Saka-Kushana' examples of Mathura. The robust features of the goddess are clearly seen. The *kanthika* worn by her is an *ekavali* of round beads, the prominent *chakra* and *makara kundalas* in the ears and the loose hair arranged centrally (a *dhammilla*) on the head and either ends shown as twigs hanging over the ear, and outstretched tongue, round eye balls and bulbous cheeks emphasize the fierceness of the Goodess in action. The upper right hand holds a *trisula* topped *danda* which pierces the forehead of the demon Mahisha. The right foot of the Goddess is placed on the head while the left is firmly planted on the ground. The lower left hand is picking up the tail of the subdued animal in a realistic way. The lower right hand is at the knee while left is holding the *Sankha*. The voluptuous yet robust and realistic female form of this goddess recalls to mind the female forms of the local Ikshvaku art. Another limestone plaque, a broken example, depicts *Viras* in a row.

Terracotta Goddess

Apart from these, a terracotta ovalish plaque depicting a peculiar female Goddess with leonine face, snake ornaments (*Sarpabhushita*) and mounted on the hood of a cobra is quite enigmatic and defies proper attribution. The outstretched legs and toes resemble that of an elephant. She holds two lilies (buds) in her uprised hands. These lilies and the voluptuous full breasts emphasize the virgin character of this cult deity. She might be a Nagini or a *Prithivi-devata*, a cult which appears to be alien to the Vengi region.

The above described cult objects bring to the fore the need to document carefully the post-Ikshvaku non-Buddhist art relics. The above pieces throw light on the obscure phase of an early Brahmanical religion which survived in Andhradesa despite the prolific Buddhist faith. Although Mahayana Buddhism dominated the art and architecture and spread its creeds far and wide, the Vedic and Brahmanical cults did not disappear. The above cult objects from the Salankayana levels at Peddavegi are thus important indicators of the Brahmanical creed.

Among the minor antiquities of Phase-IA mention has to be made of cubical dice of terracotta, ear-ornaments (*chakra* and *pushpa kundalas*) besides, tabular dice and combs of ivory. The latter recall the Kshatrapa Satavahana examples. The pottery wares right from the earliest levels of Period-IA included only dull red ware, red slipped ware and a few Red Polished Ware sprinklers and cups. There is total absence of Rouletted and the Black-and-red wares at the site. This then clearly point out that the earliest habitational activity of the historical period within the fortified area is of post-Ikshvaku date. Salankayanas made Vengi their seat of power only from the beginning of the 4th century A.D. and not earlier.

Finds from Phase IB

In the next Phase-IB, with the advent of Vishnukundins the *Stupa* was relegated to background and emphasis was laid on building Brahmanical temples of brick and stone. A *panchayatana*, closer to the *stupa* was provided with the water-chutes for draining *abhishekajala*. The pottery of the earlier Phase-IA, continued but other notable finds which clearly seperate the phase from the preceding one are the copper plated circular iron coins of the Vishnukundins besides, temples of brick. Foundations of a square *garbhagriha* were brought to light at PVG-I *stupa* site itself. An upper part of a Harihara image was found within this shrine. The robust face, wide eyes and prominent pout recall the Ajantan images of the Vakataka period. Several other architectural and sculptural components of reddish or buff or soft red sandstone were found.

Baked clay Ganesas

Notable among the cult objects of this phase were the two Ganesa figures of baked clay. Both the examples are identical in size and are in seated posture. The first one is hand modelled and measured 7cm high and 6 cm wide, has no slip and somewhat crudely finished. Two-handed with typical elephant head and ears, seated-at-ease on wide spread animal hips over a flattish *pitha* which is 6 cm square, the short stumpy legs of the deity in *ardhaparyankasana*, the trunk gently turns to right and touches the object held, perhaps an eatable, in the right palm. The left hand rests on the knee and holds a *modaka*. Except a rolled cloth on the forehead and girdle (*Sirastraka* and *vastra-mekhala*) no ornamentation exists. There is no *yajnopavita*. Mouse is also absent. Hence he can be regarded as a Bala Ganesa. There is a mortise hole on the underside of the base extending to a depth of 2.5 cm. This is meant for placing the deity over a pedastal or an upright of wood. The inner roughened part lends support to this surmise. In contrast to this example the other figure, of the same height and breadth (7 cmx62 cm) has the base of 5.3 cm square with a mortise hole for mounting it on a pedastal. It has a better finish and coloured in black slip, all over. Apart from the well marked animal eyes, a decorative cloth cover (*sirastraka*), the elephant ears are shown incised. The circular wristlets (*valayas*) as also the three-stringed *yajnopavita* in the usual *upavita* fashion clearly point out that this Ganesa is a *praudha* whose *upanayana samskara* was accomplished. Strikingly enough the toes are elephant like, the *nabhi* (navel) and the breast part are distinguished by applique pellets which were pricked with dots. It appears that the popular cult of *Ganesa pratima* made of clay, on the same lines as today, was practiced by the people during 5th century A.D. Such smaller or Bala Ganesas of reddish well-burnt clay and also in stucco and without consort but wearing *yajnopavita* are found in Maharashtra[18] and Andhra right from the later Satavahana times i e. 2nd century A.D. It is known from the pillar inscription at Velpuru (near Sattenapalli, Guntur District) that the Vishnukundin King Madhavavarman-II during his 33rd regnal year corresponding to A.D. 489 consecrated (*pratishthapitah*) a *pratima* of *Dantimukha Svami*. Interestingly this inscription ends with adoration to God Vinayaka—*Vinyakam namasyanti*.[19] This is the earliest known epigraphical citation which refers to a seperate shrine for *Ganapati* as an indepe ndent God (*Svayam pradhana murti*), not merely a nich figure (*Koshthadevata*) or subsidiary deity (*avarana devata*) as generally known to us from many places in India.

Vishnu Temple: Phase-IC (*circa* Early 7th cent. and later)

As a result of careful exposition, finer architectural details and decorated base mouldings of a stone temple dedicated to the Vishnu were brought to light at the western part of the village. The earliest phase of the temple belongs to the times of the Salankayanas who were devotees of *Chitraratha Svami* (Suryanarayana) and according to the copper plate inscriptions of the time of Nandivarman II (420-430), this temple was known as *Trailokyanatha Vishnugriha*[20]. Documentation of loose sculptures within the village revealed certain important i cons, most unique being an almost life-size Ekadaṣa-mukha Rudra with 11-heads and 24-hands armed with weaponry, Kalabhairava, Chandikesa, Suryanarayana and flying Garuda assignable to *circa* 6th and early 7th centuries A.D.

The Paramesvara temple in the midst of the village, now under worship, was freed from later accretions covering its basement and wall parts. This clearence brought to light ornate pilasters (*kudya stambhikas*) with naga brackets, a realistic Nandi or *gomukha pranala* at the northern side wall above the *prati* of the *adhisthana* of this temple which is a unique example, in this region. The temple is datable to *circa* 10th-11th century A.D.

References

1. Ramesan, N. (ed.) *Andhra Pradesh District Gazetteers : West Godavari*, Hyderabad, 1979, p.p. 20, 26-27. For a different interpretation of 'Benagauron' and also Ptolemy's 'Salakenoi' see Gopalachari K. *Early History of the Andhra country*, Madras 1976, p.p. 169-170.

2. Country of the Salankayanas mentioned so in the Ganapatha of Panini, Sircar, D.C. *Successors of Satavahanas in Lower Deccan,* Calcutta 1930. p.p. 83-84. According to Sanskrit lexicons Trikandadesa and Medini means Nandin, the attendant of Siva and Nandi becomes the *lanchana* of Salankayanas.

3. Mc Crindle, *Ancient India as described by Ptolemy,* Majumdar and Sastri (ed), pp. 67, 68 and 172.

4. Subramanian, K.R. *Buddhist Remains in Andhra and the History of Andhra between 225 and 610 A.D.*, Madras 1932, pp. 136-138; also Schoff, Welfred H. *The Periplus of the Erythrean Sea,* 2nd Edition, New Delhi 1974, p. 252.

5. Recently Dr. S.P. Tiwari of the Allahabad Museum, presented a paper at the 13th session of the Epigraphical Society of India (19-4-1987) held at the K.P. Jaiswal Research Institute, Patna. The inscription reads "*Amachasa Sa'ankayana Bhutilasa Putasa bhayaya Payovilasa miyikaya hidaya piyaya kulakam*"; see my article in Telugu *Kausambi Nagaramu numdi Salankayana Sasanamu : Vijaya Vengipura Charitrapai Konni nutanamsamulu, Bharati, Sarasvatanubhandhamu :* Vijayawada 17-6-1987.

6. Sircar, D.C. *Select Inscription,* Vol. 1, New Delhi edition, 1986, p. 265 note 1, Fleet, J.F. *Corpus Inscriptionum Indicarum* III, p. 7 line 20; see for a latest view of Samudragupta's military conquests, Buddha Prakash, Samudragupta's Southern Campaign *Prof. K. A. Nilakanta Sastri Felicitation Volume,* Madras 1971, pp. 15-37.

7. Sircar, D.C. *Asokan Studies,* Indian Museum, Calcutta 1979, pp. 121-122.

8. *Annual Report, Archaeological Survey* of *Madras,* 30th April 1888, no. 457 Public. pp. 9, 13-16. Extract from para 5 at p. 15 Sewell noticed—"All these had been removed for the canal on the south-west side of the circular trench was a white marble slab about 5 feet by 3 feet with a "Tiger" sculptured on it; it was also removed. Some bricks and stones lie around. The ring of stones might have been the base of a stone faced *Stupa*......... The excavators had simply carried round the trench so as to enable them to remove the circular ring of built masonry, and had not attaked the bank of earth which surrounds it. The white marble slab would, I believe, form a portion of the rail, and they had unfortunately come on it carrying their trench just a little too far into outer bank at this point".

9. Govt. of Madras, nos. 827-829, Public 25th August, 1902, p. 19 being the *Annual Archaeological Survey Report for the year* 1901-1902.

10. *Indian Archaeology—A Review* 1985-86 and 1986-87 (Under print). The team that worked here inclued myself and Sri G. V. Sreenivasa Rao, Dy. Superintending Archaeologist, assisted by Sarvasri S. K. Lekhwani, S. K. Mitra, Vijay Lanjewar, K. Padmanabha, J. N. Gandhi, Mohinder Singh, S. V. Sutone, P. M. Bhope, M. U. Qureshi, H. J. Bara Patre, N.K.S. Sharma, B. K. Rudra and A. V. Ganar, all belonging to the Excavation Branch (I) Nagpur.

11. Rao, N. Lakshminarayana in *Madras Epigraphical Reports, Southern Circle,* p. 219 of 1927.

12. Sarma, I.K. Epigraphical Discoveries at Guntupalle, *Journal of the Epigraphical Society of India,* V, Mysore, 1978 pp. 49-50.

13. Sarma, I.K. Brahmi Inscriptions from Vengipura Excavations, 1986-87, *Journal of the Epigraphical Society of India,* Dharwad 1987, Vol. 14.

14. Sarma I.K. A Carnelian Intaglio from Vengipura, *Prof. A.M. Shastry Felicitation Volume,* New Delhi 1987.

15. Mukherjee, B.N. *Nana on Lion—A Study in Kushana Numismatic Art,* Calcutta 1969, Appendix-II, pp. 71-73 and also 13.

16. Sarma, I.K. *The Development of Early Saiva Art and Architecture,* New Delhi 1982, pp. 148, 155-159. Photos. 39, 86.

17. Sarma, I.K. Early Historical Vestiges at Vijayawada and Some Trimurti Cult plaques; *Itihas,* Vol. VII, no. 2, Hyderabad 1979 pp. 23-31.

18. Karl Khandalvala (ed.). *Dawn of Civilization in Maharashtra,* Bombay 1975, Fig. 63 last row.

19. *Epigraphia Indica,* XXXVIII, pp. 128-129.

20. *Journal of the Andhra Historical Research Society,* Vol. I, pp. 97-98.

5

Excavations at Sannati : 1986-87*

A. Sundara

Discovery

Sannati, in Chitapura Taluka of Gulbarga District, is a pilgrim centre known for Shri Chandralamba temple. As early as 1954 the late Kapatral Krishna Rao of Gulbarga noticed here an ancient site with numerous sculptures representing symbolically main episodes of Buddha's life such as *Vajrasana* with *Budhapada* under the *Bodhivriksha*, memorial panels and numerous Brahmi inscriptions, all of 1st and 2nd century A.D., and reported about them.[1] Later Dr. S. Nagaraju in 1964 explored the area once again. This was followed by further explorations and studies by Dr. M. Sheshadri, Dr. M. S. Nagaraja Rao[3] of the Directorate of Archaeology and Museums, Mysore and Dr. P.B. Desai[4] of the Kannada Research Institute, Karnataka University, Dharwad. It may be noted here that there is on other site so rich in Buddhist relics in Karnataka, known so far, as Sannati.

Explorations

This extensive single-culture site of early historical period, roughly more than 200 hectares in area, is located on the left bank of the river Bhima near its eastward bend and is enclosed within a brick fortification wall approximately 4 m wide and 2 to 3 m high. It is divided into two parts. The part right on the bank of the river, nearly about 80 hectares in area, is prominently high and locally known as Ranamandala. The rest of the site is in a low level. About 3 km away form this site are two stately mounds which are probably Buddhist *stupas*. Near the river bank are the remains of the dislodged circular basement (of limestone slabs) of an once existing *stupa*.

Earlier many interesting sculptures, inscriptions, terracotta figurines of varieties and forms, stylistically of 1st and 2nd centuries A.D., have been collected from this site and reported. During his explorations the present author noticed on the surface of the entire site abundant quantities of pottery, roof-tiles, bricks, pieces of solid terracotta brick red pillar-like object, beads, bangles, etc. Here and there clusters of tiles, inseparably joined hard to one another while in the kiln, owing to the mineral contents of the clay used, occur indicating the local manufacture of tiles for roofing as well as remnants of brick structures. Besides, pottery pieces of grey ware fabric in varying shades of the medieval period also occur in considerable quantities. Limestone sculptural pieces are very sparingly found on the site.

The Present Study

With a view to understanding the potentialities of the site through exploration and small-scale excavation for further large-scale excavation of this important town site with Buddhist relics of the beginning of the Christian Era, the Directorate of Archaeology and Museums, Government of Karnataka, carried out preliminary studies in the site during middle December 1986—May 1987.

The brick fortification about 3.00 to 4.00 m. wide at the base and visibly 2.00-4.00 m high is still strong and massive. At two or three spots there are indications of entrances. The cultural debris is spread in considerable thickness right upto the fortification wall as revealed in some of the pits dug by local people exposing the lower part of the wall. Apparently it looks as though the fortification was raised some time after the commencement of the habitation here. The relative position of these two is yet to be ascertained. Near the river, on both sides, are found a few Middle Palaeolithic tools made on jasper, coarse carnelian, etc. A neolithic ground axe with pointed butt end, of the common type, was also picked up. Many sculptural and *stupa*-architectural pieces are found scattered all over the site, but mostly near the temple.

The area selected for the excavation is located on the south-west corner on the steeply sloping edge of the Ranamandala site near the river bank. Here was a deep rain gully with a few *jalli* trees. In the deep rain gully was exposed what looked like a cross-section of a massive wall. It seemed that the low wall like structure ran west-east along the sloping edge of the elevated site. It was, therefore, presumed that the structure visible in the rain gully was a part of perhaps an inner citadel wall. A portion of this slopy area deeply undulating owing to the rain gully and annual erosion on the river side was selected. It was divided into 24 quadrants of 5 sq. m each.

The Excavations

The quadrants were excavated to various depths from 10 cm to 2.50 m Those on the right side of the structure were found to contain no cultural debris but contained essentially the black soil. Only 4 quadrants give a complete idea of the full stratigraphy of the excavated area. They are B1, Quadrants 1-2 and C1, quadrants 1 and 3. In tl e 2.50 m thick cultural deposit, a large brick structure, a part of which lies exposed in the rain gully, and a part of another brick structure, were noticed.

Stratigraphy and Structural Remains

The cultural deposit could be divided into four layers; all of the early historical period.

Layer 1 consists of surface humus in the uppermost part and a thin bedding of limestone chips perhaps of floor level in the middle part. The debris is dirty, blackish dull brown and rather compact. Small brick pieces are found occasionally.

Layer 2 is reddish brown and ashy with ash streaks, floor levels and brickbats, charcoal bits, etc. The floor levels consist of greyish black sticky fine clay. A post-hole with remains of thin bark of a wooden pole was also noticed.

Layer 3 is similar to the above but rather more reddish brown in colour.

Layer 4, overlying the natural greyish black clay soil, is exceedingly ashy with a lot of charcoal bits and is rather loose without brickbats. Floor levels of the type noticed in the upper layer were found at places.

Squares B2, Qd 2-3; C1, Qds 3-4; and C2 revealed almost entirely, a brick structure, a part of it already visible in rain gully. A part of another structure was found in C2, Qd. 3. A noteworthy discovery is a small hearth, probably of a coppersmith in the layer 4 of B1, Qd.2.

From the contents of lyaer 4, it is evident that originally sometime after occupying the site the inhabitants provided their dwellings with clay flooring, etc. and wooden superstructure. It was only some time later people began constructing buildings in bricks, as evidenced by the contents of layer 3. This was continued till the end of the habitation.

In all the layers pottery is found in profusion. The red ware is more in quantity than the black-and-red ware in the uppermost layer and in the lower layers they are more or less equal in proportion. The pottery is of the usual fabrics and types similar to those found in other sites like Maski, etc. However, the Russet Coated White painted sherds occur on the surface very sparsely; it is not found in the excavations. There are a few potsherds of very fine core, probably of a Rouletted ware dish. Among the pottery of layer 1 was found a small piece of neolithic burnished grey ware of coarse fabric.

The Cultural Relics and Dating

Among the pottery types, large thick jars with heavy beaded rim; vases with externally beaded or thickened having an undercut or collared rim and globular body of bright red ware; cups with flat bottom, flaring undulated sides and featureless edge of coarse red ware; bowls with round bottom, vertical sides and featureless edge; shallow dishes with flat bottom, slightly convex sides and flattened edge in black and red ware are most common. In types and fabrics these are intimately akin to those of the early historical period of Maski, Chandravalli, etc.

As many as 85 beads of various shapes made on black and red jasper, carnelian, crystal, opal (?) and of glass, copper and terracotta (which predominates), are found mostly in B1 and C1 squares, i.e. behind the large structure exposed, more or less evenly in the 2nd-4th layers. About four Satavahana potin coins and two what looks like punch-marked coins (highly encrusted) were obtained from the layers mainly of Sq. C1, Qd, 1 and B1, Qd. 2 behind the structure. Within the structure these antiquities are scarcely found.

The characteristics of these excavated remains, especially the pottery, in comparison with those of Maski,

Chandravalli, etc. suggest a date range of 2nd cent. B.C-2nd cent. A.D. for the habitation here.

Thus the site appears to have a long cultural history of the human habitation, at least from the Middle Palaeolithic times preceding its rise into prominence as an important trade centre, as is evident from the memorial panel sculptures (*Chhaya padima*) depicting wealthy donors and the devout merchants who died there.

The vast extent of the site with fortification, its location, and exceedingly enormous quantities of the cultural relics of varieties and brick structural remains, sculptures, inscriptions of essentially 1st-2nd cent A.D. indicate that there must have been a town with flourishing trade attracting rich merchants patronising Budhist religion and art It is worth noting here that about 250 km north-north-west of Sannati is Ter, ancient Tagara an important trade centre, known for its cultural relies, particularly the ivory figurines of 1st-2nd cent. A.D. Likewise, about 300 km south of the place is Chandravalli with the remains of a 1st-2nd cent. township having trade contact with the Roman world. It appears, therefore, that the location of Sannati on the main trade route was one of the factors for its rise into prominence.

The Brick Structure

The extant dilapidated brick structure exposed right from the surface measures on the exterior 9.60 m long, 6.90 m broad and 3.95 m high from the bottom to the top of the maximum extant portion. The roof had completely collapsed and much of it had disappeared. The roof tiles in quantities were found fallen inside the rooms The front part had also been considerably damaged. From the present top, the floor level is 2.35 m. Obviously, the part of the structure below the floor is strikingly high; and the structure has been raised on a platform. On the front side this height is clearly visible. This platform consists of 15 courses of bricks. The structure raised on the massive platform consists of a central corridor with a series of small squarish rooms on both the sides. There might have been a few more adjacent rooms on both the sides further frontwards approched by a flight of steps. The length of the structure has not been ascertained.

There are four rooms, 1.75 m square to 1.90 x 1.50 m each on the sides of the corridor of 70 cm wide. The rooms are connected by plain openings in the partition and front walls serving as entrances of 0.60m wide; the openings varying in numbers. Interestingly enough the floor of the rooms slightly higher than the corridor, excellent and strong and is made of river sand and lime mortar laid on river pebble bedding which in turn, is on similar sand-lime mortar base. The rooms do not have windows.

In the last room on the left side of the corridor, is a flight of steps leading to the flat wide top of the thick walls. The building, therefore, appears to have been single storeyed.

Both the platform and the building are constructed in what is generally described as English bond method But in the floor of the central corridor forming the top course of the platform, the bricks are laid obliquely at an angle about 45° to the wall of the rooms above probably to increase the stability of the structure and to give an effect of an attractive simple floor design. The exterior wall of the building on the three sides is unusually and enormously thick (1.50—2.70m approximately). The bricks are mainly of two sizes 55 x 27 x 8 cm and 38 x 19 x 6 cm. The walls within the rooms were lime plastered. Outside the building near the right hand corner, is a circular wall (?) and belongs to the midlate phase of the habitations i.e. 1st cent. A.D. It is indeed of a rare type in plan and construction.

Within the rooms are found, curiously enough, heavy stone balls besides a few pottery pieces and roof tiles.

The building does not seem to be a temple or a residence because of the absence of icons and platforms etc., besides domestic articles, and the small area of the rooms adds weight to this proposition. But the stone balls found in the rooms are interesting. The balls do not have any continuance for grip so that they may be deemed as weight for weight lifting. They do not seem to be missiles of war either. Possibly they might be weighing stones of different denominations. Besides, the extraordinary security to the building indicated by the unusual thickness of the side walls and of the strong flooring seem to be indicative of the building being a warehouse of trading commodities of value, But the area of the rooms, the width of the corridor and of the entrances are too narrow for the transport of any commodities. That the rooms may be guard rooms or quarters for workers, is not tenable again because of the narrow space for movement. More data is necessary for ascertaining the correct purpose of the building.

The other building, a small part of which is exposed, is relatively later.

The Coppersmithy

A very important discovery is a small hearth, roughly circular in plain containing lots of ash, charcoal bits, copper ingots and also terracotta pipe meant for blowing air to the hearth indicating copper working and is datable to *circa* 2nd cent. B.C.

Other Cultural Remains

A miniature art motif of *stupa* railing with the depiction of a wagon vaulted hall and a tree on the sides in bold relief is worth noting. A fine heavy glass disc ear-ornament (about 5.5 cm in diameter), a large red jasper spherical bead (3.5 cm in diameter), flat tortoise shell bead, a terracotta tapering cylindrical pendant are particularly noteworthy.

References

*Revised version of this article was presented in the First Annual Congrees of Karnataka Academy in 1987.

1. Rao, Kapataral Krishna, Shri Chandrala Paramesvari, *Karnataka Samskritiya Samshodhane* (A collection of his articles reprinted), Usha Sahitya Male, Mysore. 1970, pp.252 f 2

2. Seshadri M.S. Buddhist Monuments at Sannati, *Quarterly Journal of Mythic Society*, Vol. LVI, Bangalore pp. 35—37; Buddhist Monuments in Mysore, *Artbus Asiae*, Vol. XXXIV, No. 213.

3. Nagaraja Rao M.S. *Progress of Archaeology in Karnataka: 1956-72*, Directorate of Archaeology and Museum, Mysore 1985, pp. 35—36; also Brahmi Inscriptions and their Bearing on the Great Stupa at Sannati, *Indian Epigraphy: its bearing on the History of Art*, American Institute of Indian Studies, Varanasi, pp. 41—45.

4. Desai P.B., A New Buddhist Centre, *Journal of the Karnataka University* (Soc. Sciences), Vol. IV, Dharwad pp. 3-8.

6

Vanga and Vahlika

K.D. Bajpai

In the Mehrauli iron pillar inscription are recorded the achievements of king Chandra, generally identified with Chandragupta II of the Gupta dynasty. The inscription is written in Brahmi script of the early Gupta period. The first verse of the inscription runs thus :

> यस्योद्वर्तयतः प्रतीपमुरसा शत्रुन्समेत्यागतान्,
> वंगेष्वाहववर्तिनोऽभिलिखिता खड्गेन कीर्तिर्भुजे ।
> तीर्त्वा सप्तमुखानि येन समरे सिन्धोर्ज्जिता वाह्लिकाः,
> यस्याद्याप्यधिवास्यते जलनिधिर्वीर्यानिलैर्दक्षिणः ॥

This passage means to say that king Chandra inflicated a crushing defeat on the enemies assembled in the Vanga country. He also conquered in battle the Vahlikas having crossed the seven mouths of the river Sindhu (Indus).

Here two important geographical names Vanga and Vahlika, occur. Scholars have generally identified Vanga with the eastern Bengal and Vahlika with Bactria beyond Hindukush. For instance, Dr R. C. Majumdar writes :

"Vanga denotes eastern Bengal, very nearly the same country as Samatata which is included in the tributary frontier states of Samudragupta. We do not know whether there was a rebellion in East Bengal, or whether the war was caused by the aggressive imperial policy of Candragupta which sought to incorporate the province into the dominions directly administered by him... We may well presume that his victorious arms penetrated as far as the eastern limits of India and beyond Hindukush to the north-west."[1]

Dr B.C. Law thinks that the earliest epigraphical reference to Vanga (E. Bengal) finds place in the above Mehrauli inscription.[2] He further says that "the Vahlikas should be identified with the *Bactrioi* occupying the country near Archosia in Ptolemy's time."[3]

Professor D.C. Sircar thus writes about the Vahlika country : "Vahlika country is certainly the modern Balkh region on the Oxus in the northern part of Afghanistan".[4] He thinks that the Mehrauli inscription contains an allusion to the *Chakravarti kshetra.* He takes 'Vanga' of the inscription in the sense of Bengal (representing the eastern boundary of India).[5]

The Mehrauli inscription refers to some of the exploits of Chandra in the same manner as the Allahabad pillar inscription narrates (in a much more detailed way) the achievements of emperor Samudragupta. From reliable sources we know that Chandragupta II defeated and finally extinguished the Saka-Kshatrapa families of Malwa, Gujarat and Kathiawar. This was done at a later stage of his reign, as it is proved by the inscriptional and numismatic evidence.

In the beginning, Chandragupta seems to have concentrated his strategy and energies on crushing the foreign powers, which had not been adequately dealt with by his father Samudragupta. Two such major foreign powers in India at the end of the 4th century A.D. were : (i) The Saka-Kshatrapas of eastern and western Malwa, Gujarat and Kathiawar, and (ii) the foreign rulers of Sind, Baluchistan, parts of Punjab and Kashmir. Under the second category were included the Pahlavas and the later Kushanas, having their branches settled in different parts of the region mentioned above.

It is known that king Chandragupta I of the Gupta dynasty ruled over the limited area, roughly comprising the present eastern U.P. and some parts of the contiguous areas. From the Allahabad pillar inscription of Samudragupta we learn that among the eastern kingdoms, subdued by Samudragupta, were Samatata, south-east Bengal and the major parts of Assam. Thus almost the entire Bengal was included in the domain of Samudragupta.[6]

During the reign of Chandragupta II we do not know of any political trouble, worth mention, in the eastern parts of his empire. The contemporary epigraphical and numismatic evidence is silent about any major power in the Bihar-Bengal area during the time of that ruler. It is, therefore, beyond comprehension that Chandragupta II should have thought it necessary to fight against any confederacy (?) of rulers in Bengal, the major parts of which had already been included in the Gupta empire.[7] The Allahabad pillar inscription mentions the names of several kings ruling over the areas of present Uttar Pradesh and Madhya Pradesh. Names of several rulers of south-east India are also mentioned in that record. Not a single name of the chiefs of modern eastern Bihar or of Bengal-Assam occurs there. It is, therefore, certain that Chandragupta II had not to wage any battle, worth the name, against any of his contemporary Bengal chiefs. The location of Vanga of the Mehrauli inscription has to be sought for somewhere else, more so because Vanga and Vahlika find mention together in the same verse of that inscription.

In the Sabhaparva of the *Mahabharata*[8] we read the following :

समुद्रनिष्कुटे जाताः परिसिन्धु च मानवाः ।
ते वैरामाः पारदाश्च वंगाश्च कितवैः सह ॥ 9

In chapter 48, 12 of the same *parva* we have :

कायव्या दरदा दार्वाः शूरा वैयमकास्तथा ।
औदुम्बराः दुर्विभागाः पारदा वाह्लिकैः सह ॥ 12

These verses refer to the people of the north-western regions who had come to the court of Yudhisthira with various presents for him from their respective regions. The reference to the Vanga people here is of special significance. They have been mentioned alongwith the Vairamas, the Paradas and the Kitavas. They are called the trans-Indus *(parisindhu)* people. In the second verse cited above, the Vahlika are mentioned alongwith the Paradas and other tribal people.

It is not proposed here to deal with the identifications and actual locations of all these tribes mentioned in the *Mahabharata*, the relevant portion of which seems to have been composed sometime in the middle of the 2nd century B.C. We are chiefly concerned herewith the Vangas and the Vahlikas. Let us first take up the Vangas.

The Chinese pilgrim Hiuen Tsang, who visited India in the 7th century A.D., made a reference to a people whom he called Lang Kie (Ka) Lo.[9] They, according to him, were living somewhere in the Makran coast of Baluchistan. The Sanskrit rendering of the word is *Langala*, as suggested by M. Julien (Lankar' by Watters). A section of the people of the Makran coast is still known as Langar.[10] According to the rules of the Mundakhmer language, 'Lang' is interchangable into Wang or Vang.[11]

The gifts brought to Yudhishthira by the Vangas and the other tribal people of the trans-Indus region included goats, sheep, camels, asses, gold jewels and fruit preparations. These are the well-known products of the Makran coast area even in these days.

The Vangas of the Mahabharata may thus be located in the Makran coast of Baluchistan. They seem to be the people referred to in the Mehrauli inscription as having been defeated by Chandra. From the inscription it appears that the enemies of the Gupta king, who assembled in the Vanga country, were numerous. They may have represented the foreign chiefs of the Makran coast and the region around, such as the Vairamas, the Paradas, etc. The Paradas have been identified with the Parthians, who seem to have become quite strong in the trans-Indus area during the 3rd-4th centuries A.D. Some of the classical writers have referred to the fact that they occupied the Indus delta and also that they quarrelled among themselves.[12]

In the *Ramayana* (IV, 44, 13) the Paradas are placed with the Yavanas and the Sakas before the Vahlikas.[13] In the *Harivamsa* (XIII, 763-6; XIV, 775-83) they are mentioned as the degraded and despised persons. Several Puranas[14] also refer to them in similar tones. Varahamihira places them with the Vokkanas and the Ramathas among the people of the west.[15] The Paradas have been referred to as 'Paradene' by Ptolemy (VI, 21, 4) who were living in the centre of the Panjagur oasis.

In the *Mahamayuri* we come across the names of the Paradas, the Sakas and the Vahlikas.[16] The relevant passages are quoted below :

धर्मपालश्च खशेषू बाह्ल्यां चैव महाभुजाः । 94
पाराशरः पारतेषु शकस्थाने च शंकरः । 95
वेमचित्रश्च पह्लवे केतकेषु च पिंगलः । 96
पुंड्रवर्धने पूर्णमुखः करालश्चोड्डियानके । 97

It appears from the *Mahamayuri* that, like another Vanga in the west, there was probably one Pundravardhana in the west. In this work we have the mention of Pundravardhana just after the Paradas, the Sakas, the Pahlavas and the Ketakas (correct Kekayas ?). It is followed by the name *uddiyana* (udyana). Pundravardhana there does not seem to be the one in the Rajshahi district of Bengal. The context shows that it was perhaps located in the north-west.

It is acknowledged, on early reliable grounds, that several geographical names of hills, rivers, *janapadas* and towns of the north-west, mentioned in the Vedic and later literature, were adopted in other regions of the country. Some of these names travelled to the foreign lands of south-eastern and Central Asia. The case of Vanga may have been one of them. There is no doubt that in the Gupta period the designation of a part of the present Bengal was *Vanga.*

In the Poona critical edition of the *Mahabharata*, a number of geographical passages, occurring in the great epic, have been treated as interpolations. Even then some scholars rely on them as original compositions.[17]

It is wrong to think that Chandragupta II had nothing to do with the north-west. The recent discovery of a Gupta Brahmi inscription in the Chilas-Gilgit area can be referred to here. The inscription refers to Chandragupta, who can be no other than Chandragupta II.

The first eloquent verse of the Mehrauli inscription leaves no doubt on the point that the regions of Vanga and Vahlika were conquered by that ruler. The conquests of this monarch are eulogized in several Gupta inscriptions.[18]

Recently Professor S.R. Goyal has tried to show that Chandra of the Mehrauli inscription was not Chandragupta II, but Samudragupta.[19]

Prof. Goyal has based his arguments mainly on the evidences furnished by the Mehrauli inscription, the Allahabad pillar inscription and the *Garudadhvaja* coins of Samudragupta, the Udaigiri records of Chandragupta II and the work *Kavyalankara sutravritti* of Vamana. He has tried to prove that Chandragupta II, son of Samudragupta, cannot be credited to have accomplished the victories specified in the Mehrauli inscription.

Prof. Goyal rightly says that the region of Bengal had been conquered by Samudragupta and that the major parts of Bengal had been made an integral part of the empire before the accession of Chandragupta II. I myself had pointed out to this fact years ago.[20] The latter ruler had not to wage any war against Bengal. There is no definite evidence in this regard. The reference in Kalidasa[21] is applicable probably to the victory by Samudragupta in the guise of Raghu. Vanga of the Mehrauli record was not the eastern, but the western Vanga. In the *Mahabharata*, the western Vanga of the Makran coast is referred to more than once.

The recent discovery of a Gupta Brahmi inscription near Chilas in the Gilgit area is worth mention here.[22] The recently discovered inscription at Chilas refers to Chandragupta, who does not seem to be different from Chandragupta Vikramaditya. In the Allahabad pillar inscription, the campaign of Samudragupta has been described in a remarkable geographical sequence.[23] The names of the regions conquered, along with the names of rulers in most of the cases, are given. Had Samudragupta conquered the area beyond the seven mouths (or streams of the river Indus), that fact would have clearly been mentioned by Harisena in the above record. The name of the trans-Sindhu region and that of the well-known Vahlikas are conspicuous by their absence in the Allahabad pillar inscription.

There is no doubt that Samudragupta was a great conqueror and was successful in establishing himself as a *chakravarti* ruler. He was largely responsible for unification of the country, both politically and culturally. His son, Chandragupta, conquered those regions which due to obvious reasons, could not be vanquished by his father. These new conquests were of the trans-Indus region and of Gujarat and Malwa. It was he who subdued his contemporary Scytho-Parthians in the north-west and the western Kshatrapas, who were having their hegemony in the extensive areas of modern Gujarat, parts of western Maharashtra and Malwa. This ruler consolidated the great Gupta empire which lasted for a considerable time after his death.[24]

Like his illustrious father, Chandragupta Vikramaditya rightly acquired the *chakravarti* position. Even the southern powers, the Vakatakas, the Kadambas and others, acknowledged his suzerainty and his fame was spread up to the southern ocean. It is, therefore, not surprisiug that in the Mehrauli inscription a reference to the ocean is made.

Samudragupta adhered to the Vaishnava faith. But his son was through and through a Vaishnava. His title of *paramabhagavata*, his *chakravikrama* type of coinage and his numerous activities at Sanchi, Vidisha-Udaigiri, the Vishnupadagiri and other places eloquently prove that he was a great devotee of Vishnu.[25]

The reference in the work of the writer Vamana[26] may be to Samudragupta, but the term *chandraprakasa* simply means 'having the glow of moon'. It does not mean Chandra is eulogised as 'his face shining like the full moon.'

Dr Goyal has raised a pertinent question as to why the victory of Chandragupta II over the Sakas of western India does not find mention in the Mehrauli inscription. He calls this victory as 'the greatest achievement' of this ruler, with which statement it may not be possible to agree. At any rate, the absence of the mention of victory over western India in the Mehrauli inscription requires explanation.

The Mehrauli pillar inscription was most probably composed earlier than the two records of Chandragupta II, the one found at Udaigiri dated Saka 82 (A.D. 401) and the other at Sanchi dated Saka year 93 (A.D. 412). This ruler had issued his silver coins of the western Saka style after occcupying the region of Malwa and Gujarat. The earliest Saka year 90 (A.D. 409) on several silver coins of this king indicates that he conquered the Malwa-Gujarat region from the Sakas in the closing years of the 4th century A.D. The date found on the last Kshatrapa coins of this area can be bracketted between A.D. 388 and 397.[27]

No date has been found on the Mehrauli iron pillar inscription due to the obvious poetic exigency. The Mathura inscription of Chandragupta II is dated in the year 61 (A.D. 380).[28] It appears that soon after this date, he proceeded on his campaign of the north-west. It may have taken quite some time in accomplishing victory over the turbulent occupants of that area. Some idea of this campaign can be obtained from the *Raghuvamsa* (IV, 60-70) of Kalidasa.

It was due to the above reason that no mention of the victory of Chandragupta II is recorded on the Mehrauli incription, which was composed earlier than the achievement of his victory over western India. Prof. Goyal thinks that the king mentioned in the Mehrauli inscription flourished either in the second half of the 4th century or in the beginning of the 5th century A.D. The latter part of this contention cannot be valid. It was not Samudragupta but Chandragupta II who ruled in the beginning of the 5th century A.D. Had the Mehrauli pillar been set up during his reign as a posthumous record of his father, Chandragupta, for very definite reasons, would not have called his father *Chandrahva* on this prestigious iron pillar.

The question of Vahlika may now be taken up. The literary and archaeological evidence shows that the most important town of this name was located in the Oxus basin, north of the Hindukush. It is the modern Balkh in Afghanistan. It was obviously situated in the *Ketumala varsha* of the Puranas. The area around that town was also called Vahlika.

Several other towns were designated after this name. One of these was located in the modern Baluchistan, south of Quetta. Presently it is known as Balis. The region covered by the valleys of the Bolan, Nari and Gokh rivers was called Vahlika. It finds mention in several early Puranas.[29]

Another Vahlika (Vahika) was probably coterminus with the *udichyas* and was located beyond the Sarasvati river (modern Ghaggar) in the Vipasa valley. It is mentioned in the *Ramayana*.[30] Professor O.P. Bharadvaja has discussed this important passage in the great epic.[31]

Yet another town assumed the name of Vahlika (Balkh). It was the modern Bagh in the Dhar district of Madhya Pradesh, wherefrom a number of copper plates bearing the name of the town were issued.[32]

The various references to the Vahlikas in the two great epics and in the Puranas tend to show that several branches of them had migrated from their mainland beyond Hindukush to western Punjab and Baluchistan regions. A branch of them in course of time may have gone to western Malwa in the area of Bagh. The present 'Balis', south of Quetta and the Bolan pass seems to have still retained the old name of the Vahlikas.

The present study is an effort to offer identifications of the two regions Vanga and Vahlika occurring in the Mehrauli inscription. The manner in which the two names are mentioned in that record clearly shows that these two cannot be entirely unconnected from each other. As I have shown, Vanga in the inscription cannot refer to the present Bengal. Likewise, Vahlika cannot be taken to imply Bacteria in Afghanistan. Chandragupta does not seem to have carried his arms to such a distant place as the Afghan Turkistan, situated north of the Hindukush. We have no clear evidence whatsoever to prove that Chandragupta inflicted defeat on the peoples living across the Hindukush. At the most, he may have gone to the Gilgit area, in the northern direction.

In the *Mahabharata* the Vahlikas, presumably of the Punjab-Baluchistan areas, are, time and again, despised as degraded persons and such is the case with the writers of several Puranas also. This shows that they were treated as foreigners, alien to the Aryan way of life. To ward off the trouble from the north-western direction, Chandragupta may have thought it imminent to oust them from the strategic position occupied by them. To this victory a reference has aptly been made in the Mehrauli iron pillar inscription.

Prof. V.C. Pandey opines that the words '*Sindhoh Sapta-mukhani* of the inscription should not be taken in the sense of seven mouths or seven streams of the river Indus'. He prefers to take the world *Sindhu* in the sense of the *Mahabharata* (I, 169, 19-22). Prof. Pandey writes : 'The epic refers to these seven feeders of the sea on the eastern side of the Vahlika country, i.e. in Madhyadeśa. They are: 1. The Ganga, 2. the Yamuna, 3. the Sarasvati, 4. the Rathastha (Ramganga), 5. the Saryu, 6. the Gomati, and 7. the Gandaki. Since the region watered by these seven rivers lay between Vanga and Vahlika, Chandragupta II, proceeding from Vanga or his capital at Pataliputra, had naturally to march through it to reach the latter[33]."

The above view loses its ground after considering the points discussed above.

References

1. *The Classical Age*, p. 20.
2. *Historical Geography of Ancient India*, Paris 1954, pp. 267 ff.
3. *Ibid.*, p. 133.
4. *Studies in the Geography of Ancient and Medieval India*, Delhi 1960, p. 184.
5. *Ibid.*
6. *The Classical Age*, pp. 8-9.
7. R.C Majumdar surmises that before the so-called campaign of Chandragupta II over Bengal, the direct Gupta rule did not exist in Bengal. But there is no tangible evidence to support this view.
8. Critical edition (Poona), *Sabha parva*, ch 47, 9-10.
9. Watters on *Yuan Chwang* II, pp. 257-58; See also Cunningham's *Geography of Ancient India*, pp. 355-56.
10. *Baluchistan Gazetteer*, VII, p. 106.
11. See Moti Chandra, *Studies in the Upayana parva*, pp. 53-54.
12. The *Periplus* refers to Minanagara of the Indus delta ruled over by Parthian princes, who "were perpetually at strife among themselves". See Majumdar R.C., *Classical Accounts of India*, Calcutta, 1960, p. 300.
13. In the *Mbh. (Sabhaparva*, 48, 12) also the Paradas are mentioned just before the Vahlikas.
14. *Markandeya*, ch. 57, 37.
15. *Brihatsamhita*, XIV, 21.
16. Agrawala, V.S. *Journal of the U.P. Hist. Society*, Vol. XV, pp. 48 ff.
17. Pandey V.C. Vangas and the Vahlikas of the Mehrauli pill. Ins , *Vishva Bandhu Com. Volume, VIJ*, XII, pp. 1-5.
18. The Mandsaur inscription of the time of Govindagupta dated Malava year 524, verse 3. *Ep. Indica*, Vol. XXVII, pp. 12 ff.
19. Paper circulated to scholars for review. In his work *A History of the Imperial Guptas*, Allahabad 1967, pp. 201-09, Dr Goyal has expressed the same views. His new article is a slight amendment of the same.
20. Bajpai, K.D. Identification of Vanga and Vahlika. *V.V. Mirashi Volume*, Nagpur 1965, pp. 355-61.
21. *Raghuvamsa*, IV, 36-37.
22. Prof. A.H. Dani in his publication entitled *Chilas* has referred to this inscription along with a large number of Kharoshthi inscriptions incised on rocks in that area.
23. Bajpai, Some problems of Anc. Indian History, *Bulletin of Anc. Ind. History & Archaeology*, Sagar University, 1967. No. I, pp. 1-6.
24. Raychaudhuri, H.C. *Political History of Anc. India*, 7th edition, Calcutta 1972, pp. 492-8; Sircar, D.C. *Anc. Malwa and the Vikramaditya Tradition*, Delhi 1969, pp. 113-23.
25. Altekar, A.S. *The Coinage of the Gupta Empire*, Varanasi, 1957, pp. 150-52.
26. *The Kavyalankarasutravritti*, Calcutta ed., p. 85.
27. Altekar, *op. cit.* pp. 151-52.
28. Sircar, D.C. *Select Inscriptions*, Vol. I, pp. 283-85.
29. Ali, S.M. *The Geography of the Puranas*, Delhi 1967, p. 142.
30. *Ramayana* II, 62, 12; For references in the *Mahabharata*, see *Mbh.* I, 124, 21, VIII, 44, 7, etc.
31. Bharadwaj, O.P. *Studies in Historical Geography of Ancient India*, Delhi 1986, pp. 93, 97-98, 245 note 58.
32. Bajpai, K.D. *Cultural History of India*, Vol. I Delhi 1985, p. 47. Also see J. Pryzulski, *Indian Studies*, Vol. I (4), p. 729 ff.
33. Pandey, V.C. *op. cit.*, pp. 3-5.

7

Restrictions on arresting Persons : an ancient example

R. Nagaswamy

Arresting persons who commit crimes, and enquiring and imposing punishment is an essential function of the king. But there are also certain restrictions imposed on arrests. In this connection an epigraph dated A.D. 1010 from Tamil Nadu is interesting.

The inscription, in Tamil dated in the 25th regnal year of the Chola king Rajakesarivarman (Rajaraja I) is found on a pillar in the *mandapa* in front of the Varadaraja perumal temple in Kaveripakkam village, Arkonam taluk, North Arcot district. The inscription copied by the Government Epigraphist—ARE 400/1905, is published in South Indian Inscription, Volume 13, No. 312.

A brief introduction by the editor reads : "This is probably an inscription of Rajaraja I. It records some regulations banning the service of women (for conducting the festivals in the temple) as decided by the *mahasabha* of Kavidipakkam alias Avaninarayana Chaturvedimangalam in Paduvurkottam on an order received by them from the king through Venbaikkudinatturvelar. Avaninarayana is known to have been a *biruda* of Pallava Nandivarman III. We learn that the assembly comprised the committees *Urvariyam, Udasinavariyam, Erivariyam, Kalanivariyam*, the *bhattas* and *visishtas* of of the village":

The inscription is of far greater significance than mentioned by the editor.

The inscription may be divided into six parts:

(1) The king and date of the record; (2) The assembly (*mahasabha*) of the village; (3) An officer of the king arrives with the royal decision; (4) The royal decision; (5) The village assembly passes a resolution as per the royal decision; and (6) The *madhyastha* of the village drafts the resolution under the orders of the village assembly.

A translation of the inscription is given below followed by a discussion on the salient features of the record.

Inscription

1. Svasti Sri. In the 25th regnal year of the king Rajakesarivarman
2. the *mahasabha* great assembly of the village Kavidippakkam also known as Avaninarayana Chaturvedimangalam (in the subdivision Paduvurkottam) consisting of the members of *urvariyam* (the village committee), *Udasinavariyam, Erivaryam* (tank committee), *Kalanivariyam*, (cultivated-field committee), *Bhattas* (exponents of sastras), and *visishtas* (noblemen) having assembled in the *Kamakkottam* of the village
3. and having heard from Venbaikkudivelar, who arrived under the orders of *Perumanadi* (king) with the royal decision that:
4. (a) You (the *mahasabha*) are exempted from accepting any instrument of legal action (*karana*) on either the fullmoon day (*uva*), the first day of the bright fortnight (*pratipat*) or the *sankranti* day;

   (b) In case any such instrument of action is served no male (*purushas*) or female member (*strikal*) should be taken to village assembly hall (or court-*ambalam*);

   (c) Those who take women (in contravention of this decision to the assembly hall) commit crime against the king and the village assembly; and

   (d) The king has ordered that, you the village assembly (*mahasabha*) pass a resolution (*vyavastha*) to this effect and have it engraved on stone (*silalekha*)
5. Having listened to Venbaikudivelar, who came to the *mahasabha* and narrated thus the members of the *sabha* resolved that :

(i) there is no need to accept any instrument of legal action served on the day of *uva*, *pratipat* and *sankranti*,

(ii) When any is served the male members (*purusha*) may be taken (arrested) to the *ambalam*,

(iii) If the male member is not to be found the womenfolk (*strikal*) should not be taken (captured),

(iv) Those who take them, do crime against the *sabha* and the king,

(v) This resolution should be enforced by the administrative officer of the village and the members of the *samvatsara variyam*, committee of the respective years (of occurrence),

(vi) Even if a royal directive is received (*Rajaniyoga*) the functions of the Government or the village *Rajakarya* and *grama karya* should not be effected (on these days), and

(vii) This is the resolution of us the members of *Mahasabha* , which included the members of the six committees of this *ambala*.

6. Under orders of this assembly, I, the *madhyastha* of this village drafted this . . . .

Import of the inscription

From the above, it is clear that the inscription, is intended to place some restriction on arrests on some specific days, in a month. The main purport of the inscription is:

(1) The village assembly is exempted from accepting any instrument of action on three days.

(2) Neither the defendant male member nor his womenfolk should be summoned to the village court on these three days.

(3) On other days, only the erring male member should be taken to the village court and

(4) In case the erring male was not found (absconding), his womenfolk *should not* be taken to the village court.

The great assembly (*mahasabha*) met in the *Kamakkottam* of the village is the important point that deserves attention. *Kamakkottam*, is a term used for the temple of goddess Parvati. In many inscriptions of the Cholas, the goddess in Siva temple is called *Kamakkottam*. In some instances, the temple of the goddess also was located outside the Siva temple complex as in the case of Kamakshi at Kanchipuram. In the worship of the goddess Kamakshi also known as Lalita, Tripurasundari and Rajarajesvari, the three days mentioned in the inscription were obviously held sacred. In Tantric worship, the *Purnima*, (*uva* in Tamil) is the most important puja and occupied a very great place is well known. So also the first day of the bright fortnight is an important day for the worship of the goddess. In the Lalita Sahasranama, the goddess is called *pratipad mukhyarakantatithi mandala Pujita*. According to Bhaskararaya, the famous commentator, the word *Pratipat* would donote *Kamesvari*

Sankaranti, a great auspicious day is also well known. Thus the three days *Purnami*, *Prathama* and *Sankranti* are venerated days for goddess, the supreme female principle. On these three days the women are worshipped as the very incarnations of the goddess by Hindus. Nothing should be done to hurt the feelings of women especially on those days. The royal decision had two important implications: (a) the feelings of women should not be hurt by arresting men on those days, as such, prohibition was imposed on serving any legal instruments of action on these days; (b) on other days if the male to be arrested was not found, the womenfolk of his family should not be taken to the village court and coerced. In all probability such a custom of taking woman to the village court to compel the male member to give himself up was prevalent and that the king prohibited this custom, by declaring such an action as a crime against the crown. Such a prohibition for not only to king's government but also to the village assembly was also directed to pass such a resolution. It was precisely for this reason the village assembly met at the *Kamakkottam* of the village which obviously played a very important role in the life of the people of this village.

Narada on Arrests

It is interesting to note that Narada in his *Dharma sastra*, mentions such prohibitions on arrests (I. 46). One arresting improperly is liable to penalty (47). One desirous of celebrating his nuptials, afflicted with an illness, about to perform a sacrifice, distressed, sued by another party, employed in the king's service (48), cowherds while tending their cattle, husbandmen in the act of cultivation, artisans, engaged in trades, soldiers engaged in warfare (49), a minor, a messanger, one about to give alms or fulfilling a vow and one surrounded by difficulties, must not be arrested by the adversary nor summoned by the king.

The above citations from Narada shows that according to ancient *Dharma sastras*, imposing restrictions on arrest of men, was well known. What the present inscription shows is the concern of the king for the protection of women and their feelings. It is an interesting example of Rajarajachola's judicial administration.

8

Indian Indonesia

C.C. Mullick

The process of Indianisation of Indonesia has been a subject of academic controversy till date. Most of the Dutch scholars always opposed the notion that India made certain impact or influenced the religion, religious art and the culture of Indonesia. One of the exponents of this view was Bosch, He wrote a long article in *Rupam* entitiled, "A Hypothesis as to the origin of Indo-Javanese Art".[1] In this comparatively long article Bosch attempted to ignore and discard the previous theories. He virtually did put aside the Kshatriya, Vaisya and Brahmin agencies, who are said to have carried, according to some scholars, Indian influences specially of Sarnath and Nalanda and to a certain extent of Ajanta to Indonesia. He regretted that "it is foolishness for the people to repeat one after another that it was the Hindus, who did everything in Java in the realm of art and the Javanese were used for coollie work. He however, appeared to have toned down subsequently his extremely critical observations made in the aforesaid article.[2] In a later article entitled "The problems of Hindu colonisation of Indonesia" he preferred the terms like 'fusion' or mixing in place of 'impact' or 'influence' of Indian religion and art on Indonesian soil. Almost similar opinion was maintained by Krom. To Krom the peaceful penetration of Indian traders and merchants in the island took place initially, who thereafter entered into relation with the natives. He established the pre-existence of an Indonesian society and its culture which came into contact subsequently with the Indian culture. The Indigenous Indonesians voluntarily accepted the so called Hindu civilization. He categorically denied that the Hindus ever conquered the native Indonesians and imposed their institution on the sudued population of Indonesia. To Krom, the process of Hinduisation in Indonesia was slow, complex and uneven.[3] Coedes termed this process as 'osmosis'.[4] However, it appears that the process of Indianisation was more active in the field of religion and religious art than any other expressions of Indonesian culture. But Clair Halt in her book *Art in Indonesia, continuities and change*,[5] includes a chapter named the 'Impact of Indian influences'. In this chapter she categorically surmised the manner in which influences penetrated into Indonesia. According to her : (1) the colonisation by the Indians combined with intermarriage between Indian princes and the daughters of local chiefs led to the Indianisation of Indonesia (Kshatriya, agency), (2) the dissemination of Indian religious ideas and technical skills from the settlements of the Indian traders paved the way for Indianisation (Vaisya agency), and (3) the Indian priests introduced Indian religion among the ancient Indonesians (Brahmin agency).

Whatever the terms a scholar would like to coin (fusion, admixture, etc.) a cursory glance on the specimens of Indonesian art would at once remind us their ancestry and their nearness or closeness with Indian art of certain schools, such as Sarnath, Nalanda, Ajanta, etc. But the question is, one has to trace beyond any doubt, the routes as well as the way, the various religious modes and artistic idioms went to Indonesia from India.[6]

The migration of religious creed and art, to a certain extent was made possible by the visiting religious teachers in Suvarnadvipa. Gunavarman of Kashmir passed Suvarnadvipa and preached Buddhism there. Dharmapala, a teacher of Nalanda stayed for a while in ancient Indonesia. Kumaraghosha, Vajrabodhi and his disciple Amoghavajra on their way to China halted for some time at Srivijaya. It appears that they were mainly responsible for preaching the various aspects of Buddhism there.[7] Scholars believe that ancient Srivijaya possibly served as the media through which Buddhist traditions of India penetrated ancient Indonesia. We know that Srivijaya in ancient times was a great centre of Mahayana Budhism.

I-tsing, the Chinese traveller was in Srivijaya in the second half of the seventh century and thousands of monks, scholars and pilgrims studying sanskrit and Sanskrit texts; and the texts were translated into other languages. Ghosh thinks that not only Sarnath, Nalanda and Ajanta but Orissa also played a significant role in migrating Indian religion and religious art to Indonesia.[8] In this connection it may be stated that the ports of Tamralipta in Bengal, Palur in Orissa,[9] and Bhrigukachchha in Gujarat served as the gateways through which Gupta and Pala artistic traditions flowed down to Indonesia.

Indian influence which up to the present day it is possible to trace in many an aspect of Javanese life has found its grandest expression in those numerous monumental and sculptural remains with which isle of Java is studded. However, it appears that the artistic trends from Indian mainland were introduced to Indonesia through small sized bronze and terracotta images and with the help of small seals and sealings inscribed with religious creed and images. The reason was obvious. These were easily portable and in all probability, these were carried back to Indonesia to a large extent by the Indonesian pilgrims and students who came to India considering it as a holy land and on their way back they had taken with them the sacred mementos of their visit to India. Some travellers might have had taken also some such portable articles, materials to Indonesia. The pious Buddhists from Indonesia, on the completion of their studies in India not only carried only one image as memento of sacred land but they appear to have carried dozens of such images belonging, perhaps, to a Kula or a Dhyani Buddha or the entire members of a Buddhist *mandala*; this explains the introduction of Mahayana, Tantrayana iconography and art in Indonesia. In this connection mention must be made of a large copper plate grant of Sridevapaladeva[10] in which king Devapala granted five villages and apparently, built a monastery in Nalanda at the instance of Sailendra king Balaputradeva for the students hailing from Suvarnadvipa.

It is further held that the priests specialised in architecture (*sthapati*) and sculptor (*sthapaka*) of India played important roles in the development of temple architecture of Borobodur, Mendut, Sewu, Kalasan and Lara-Jonggrang. These priest-architects who were well versed in Saivite and Buddhist texts used their profound knowledge of religion and religious symbolism in planning a temple or decorating the same with relief sculptures.[11] The above references are sufficient to prove that how early Indian religions and art migrated to Indonesia and made its impact felt in the religion and religious art of Indonesia. When an analysis is made to study stone and bronze sculptures in the various parts of Indonesia, it would be hardly difficult for any scholar to trace their ancetry in Indian soil. In the paragraphs below an attempt is being made to analyse some bronze and stone images of Indonesia and their close association with Indian counterparts. Barring certain ethnic elements in the facial features, the Indonesian images bear unmistakable evidences of Indianness.

The Buddhist monumets at Borobodur had in its three circular terraces, seventy-two votive *stupas* and each *stupa* has diamond shaped perforations in its body. Each of these *stupas* was installed with an image of Buddha seated in *dharmachakraprvartana mudra*. Some of these *stupas* are still intact while a number of such *stupas* have been mutilated and thereby exposed images of Buddha in *dharmacakra mudra*. While explaining the architectural symbolism, certain scholars take these circular terraces with *stupas* as representing the third stage of the way to move to the *nirvana*. The first is represented the *Kamadhatu*, the second stage delineated the *Rupadhatu* and the third stage symbolised *Ruparupa lhatu* and the final stage singified the *Arupadhatu*.[13] It is not my intention to analyse the importance of the relief sculptures of Borobodur but to trace if there are any similarities or impact on these sculptures from India. The three dimentional images of Buddha on the upper terraces at Borobodur, reminds one of the sculpture of Buddha in *dharmachakra mudra*[14] found from Sarnath, which is now kept in the Archaeological Museum at Sarnath. The images of Borobodur appears to be replicas of Sarnath Buddha image. In iconography, in its plasticity and in its feeling, the Sarnath Buddha in *dharmachakra mudra* appears to be the ancestor of the seventy two images on the circular terraces of Borobodur. Barring certain ethnic features in their faces and in the folds of the drapery below the joining of two legs in these images, there is nothing that could differenciate the Sarnath Buddha image and these images. Seated just as the Indian prototype within an isosceles triangle, the Borobodur images bear typical Javanese facial features otherwise the impact of Sarnath school is very apparent in their iconographic details and in plastic diction. Possibly the Sarnath idiom went to Indonesia with certain plastic changes through Nalanda and Ratnagiri [15] On the walls of the galleries in this so called second symbolic phase (*Rupadhatu*), one finds narrative representatives in high relief, dealing with stories from the *Lalitavistara* and *Gandavyuha*. In these reliefs, one finds images of Buddha appearing as the central figure of many narratives. The images of Buddha which are found to be carved on sectional stones show very intimate connections with the reliefs of Ajanta. The images of Buddha in these reliefs are shown standing in very graceful *tribhanga* posture, the way he stands reminds immediately of the Buddha images standing in similar posture on the facade of Cave No. 16 and 17 at Ajanta. Not only the flexion of the body but also in the treatment of drapery, the standing Buddha images in relief at Ajanta appear to have made a deep impact on the relief sculptures of Borobodur. But these standing postures of the Ajanta reliefs in their own turns imbibed inspirations from the standing Buddha images of Sarnath. Such, standing postures in the Buddha images are, curiously enough, met with certain standing images of Buddha in Nalanda and in the images found in certain parts of Bangladesh in the post-Gupta period. Hence, the notion of standing images of Buddha might have travelled to Indonesia, apart for Ajanta and also from the eastern Indian schools of post-Gupta sculptures.[16]

There are two gargozsles in the Djakarta Museum, one designed in the shape of a *makara* and the other in the shape of a *kirtimukha*. In Java, the *kirtimukha* (face of glory) motif is designated as Kalamukha or Banaspati.[17] These two mythical animals which were originally carved to drain out the water of the temples exhibit definite Indian inspiration. Such gargoyles were made from about the Gupta period in Indian and it continued thereafter.

Rijksmuseum voor Volkenkunde in Leiden, Holland, has certain images that may be taken up for discussion in this article. One of such images (No. 1403-2345) shows Buddha seated *bhadrasana* and his two hands are engaged in *dharmachakra pravartana mudra*. This image has been stylistically dated in the later half of the 9th century A.D. Its somewhat stiff limb, plump and metallic smoothness call for such a dating. Plastically it calls for a comparision with a Buddha figure in *bhadrasana* from Semarang in Central Java. Assigned to a slightly earlier date, the second image of the Buddha has been found to be conceived in similar posture ; plastically speaking, this image appears to be vacillating between classical trends of Gupta India and early eastern Indian trends of the Pala period. This image of the Buddha in the Leiden Museum (No. 1403-2844) needs a detailed analysis in order to estimate its iconographic and stylistic indebtedness to Indian Buddha images of earlier period. The Buddha is shown seated in *bhadrasana* on an artistically conceived throne; a circular halo encircles his head. The halo is severely plain in the middle and its edges all along moulded and decorated with scalloped designs. At the botton of this halo and almost behind his neck, a few flames still survive which show that the halo was originally surrounded with flames. At the top of this member, a few stylised *Asvattha* (*Ficus Religiosa*) leaves appear, symbolising the Bodhi tree under which the Master attained his final salvation. The Buddha is clad in *trichivara*, and his both shoulders are covered with his scarf (*ubhayamsika samghati*). His lower garment reaches upto his shin bones and shows a few stylised folds. His feet are kept slightly apart.

The enthroned images of the Buddha is placed on a *tri-ratha* pedestal. In front of a central projection at the base there appears a four-spoked wheel (*dharmachakra*) which is flanked on either side by the strict profiles of two deers. These two elements refer to the event of the turning of the wheel of law (*dharmachakrapravartana*) by the Buddha and point to its local *mrigadava* i.e. the deer park of Sarnath. Just behind the wheel, a comparatively thick stalk moves up culminating in a spreading full blown lotus. This lotus footstool is flanked on either side by a *gaja-simha* motif while on the two extreme projections of the base, two open mouthed lions are shown seated on their haunches. On either side of the throne on which the Buddha is shown seated, a decorative motif has been very carefully and artistically adjusted. The motif includes at its bottom a couchant elephant in profile, a dwarfish rider on it in the middle and the latter is surmounted by a standing *simha-vyala*. A knobbed cross-bar from the back rest of the throne projecting to the left is mutilated. From the right side knobbed projection hangs a narrow and designed strip which is found to be divided into three registers inscribed with a common motif which, however, is difficult to identify.

These elements in its decorative detail betray strong Indian symbol and the parallel is taken from the clay seals of the Pala period.[18] The knobbed cross-bar projected on either side of the throne is very commonly found design on Pala bronzes at Nalanda (eg. Buddha image in Patna Museum, Acc. No. 4859 and *cf*. Hariti image in National Museum, New Delhi, Acc. No. 681712). The *simha-vyala* or *simha* standing on a couchant elephant is also noticed in Nalanda bronzes.[19] The Indonesian bronze casters introduced a dwarfish male in between the *simha-vyala* and the couchant elephant. But introduction of this dwarf in this way was not a novel addition by the Indonesian sculptor. Dwarfish male figure riding a couchant elephant and either side of a seated Buddha was introduced earlier in India. On a votive *stupa* at Ajanta, similar elements are noticed where Buddha is shown seated in *bhadra-*

sana and his hands are in *dharmachakra mudra*. On either side of this image, a counchant elephant, a rider and a *simha-vyala* are noticed but Ajanta has another rider on the back of *sima-vyala* which, however, is not the case in the Indonesian bronze Buddha. Kempers thinks that the delineation of *simha-vyala* may be traced as early as the Gupta Sarnath.

On the Ajanta votive *stupa* and near the legs of the seated Buddha there appears on either side *gaja-simha* motif. The *gaja-simha* motif on Indonesian bronze Buddha was conceived in profiles but Ajanta went for somewhat different composition. At Ajanta, the fore-part of an elephant was treated frontally while the triumphant lion on it treated in profile. Moreover, the Ajanta lions are shown seated on elephants with a majestic grandeur but Indonesian lions in *gaja-simha* motif appeared in the action of breaking the skull of elephants.

The halo behind the head of the bronze Buddha also requires certain consideration. The general contour of the halo in this image of Indian Museum recalls the halo behind the image of Buddha at Candi Mendut. The Mendut halo is severely plain and has ogee pointed finial. This shape reminds one, the halo behind the head of the Buddha enshrined within the niche worked out on the votive *stupa* at Ajanta, Cave No. XXVI. The halo, in this case is also plain and moves to a pointed finial which however, could not be accomodated entirely by the sculptor due to the paucity of space. Hence the halo at Ajanta may be said to have inspired Mendut carver and then in general shape and in contour line, in its own turn, it influenced the bronze Buddha. But the flames that encircle the halo of the bronze Buddha were noticed earlier in many Pala bronzes (cf. Nalanda Buddha in Patna Museum No. 8459).

Besides these decorative detalls, when compared in terms of plastic realisations, these bronze Buddha images bear strong resemblences with earlier Indian Buddha types. In fact, the nucleus of all these Buddha images, discussed earlier, may be traced in a Sarnath image of Buddha seated in *bhadrasana*[20] whose hands are in *dharmachakra mudra*. Conceived against a plain *prabhavali*, this image of fifth century A.D., made of Chunar sandstone and a unique collection of British Museum, London, appears to have served as the model for such type of subsequent images within and without India.

Sarnath idiom of the Gupta period reverberated in the peripheral areas. Cave no. XXVI at Ajanta in the late 5th century followed the plastic diction of the aforesaid British Museum Buddha. Illumined from within, shining a *prajna*, and immersed deep within itself[22] this Sarnath image made a deep impression not only on the stone carvers at Ajanta, but inspired to a great extent the artists working in subsequent Nalanda. The sculptures of Nalanda made a tremendous impact on the subsequent development of art in Nepal and Tibet on the one hand and Indonesia on the other. It appears that Nalanda initially got its inspiration from its neighbour, the sculptural repertoire of Sarnath and then in its own turn, it made its influence felt in Indonesia. Aajanta Cave no. XXVI and its art appears to have been compromised while carving the colossal Buddha image at Mendut in the 8th century A.D. Serenely beautiful the Buddha at Candi Mendut in Indonesia, represents the classic Indo-Javanese art.[23] The bliss and serenity are the two essential features of Mendut Buddha. These features travelled to Mendut from Sarnath *via* Ajanta. The bronze Buddhas in Leiden Museum were produced after Mendut as its miniature replicas. Of the two bronzes, while one (No. 1408-2844) vacillates between Gupta and Pala idioms, the second one (No. 1403-2845) has completely surrendered to the eastern Indian idioms of the Pala period.

References

1. Bosch, F.D.K. A hypothesis as to the origin of Indo-Javanese Art, *Rupam*, 17, 1924, p. 41.
2. Stutterheim, W.F. *Studies in Indonesian Archaeology*, The Hauge, 1961. "I found among the remains of Nalanda something that may be recognised as the immediate models of Central Javanese Art".
3. Krom, N.J. *Sumatran Period of Javanese History*.
4. Coedes, G. *L' osmos Indienne en Indochine et en Indonesie cahiers d' Histiore Mondiale*, I, 1954, pp. 837-838.
5. Halt, Clair. *Art in Indonesia, continuities and change*, Cornell University Press, Ithaca, New York 1976, pp. 35-36.
6. Majumdar, R.C. *Classical Age*, Bombay 1954, p. 144.
7. Ghosh, D.P. Indonesia : Past and present, *Amrit Bazar Patrika, Puja Annual*; also Coomaraswamy and South East Asian Art paper read in Coomaraswamy Centenary Seminar, organised by the Centre of Advance Study, Deptt. of AIHC & ARCH., Calcutta University.
8. *Ibid*.
9. Mahatab, H. *The History of Orissa*, Radhakumud Mukherjee Endowment lecture, C. VII, Lucknow University, 1947, pp. 39-41.

10. Majumdar, R.C. *The Age of Imperial Kanauj*, Bombay 1955, p. 52; also *The struggle for Empire*, Bombay 1957, p. 130 and *Hindu Civilization in South East Asia.*
11. Bosch, *op. cit.* pp. 54-57.
12. Gomez, L. and Woodword. *Barabudur, History and significance of a Buddhist monument*, California 1981, pp. 4-5 and 116.
13. Stutterheim 1961. *op. cit.*
14. Coomaraswamy, A.K. *History of Indian and Indonesian Art*, Delhi 1972, p. 85; also Sherman E. Lee. *A History Far Eastern Art*, London 1964, p. 107.
15. Mullick, C.C. Nalanda Sculptures : Its bearing on Indonesian Sculptures; Ph. D. Thesis (unpublished) B.H.U., Varanasi, 1986.
16. Agrawal, V.S. *Studies in Indian Art*, Varanasi 1965, pp. 98-99. *Makara* and *Simsumarasirah* are synonymous. The Head of the fish-tailed *makara* occupied the ends of the architrave beams in early Indian Art, the well known motif of the ancient gateways in India as well as in the Indonesian architecture. Sometimes *makara* motif represented with coiled fish-tail and a gaping mouth or '*karala-mukha*'; also Kramrisch, Stella. *The Hindu Temple*, Vol. II, Delhi 1976 and Rowland, Benjamin. *The Art and Architecture of India*, 1967.
17. Kempers, A.J. Bernett. *Hindu Javanese Bronzes*, Lecture delivered in Indian Society, Jan. 24, 1934.
18. Hussain, Shahanara, *Everyday life in Pala Empire*, Dacca 1968, p. 68; also Stutterheim, *Rama Legenden and Rama relief in Indonesia*, Munche 1925, p. 215. "Relation of Nalanda and Sailendra dynasty in Java has been clearly disclosed by the Nalanda charter of king Devapala. Bala putra asked for a grant of five villages for the upkeep of an Indonesian monastery to accommodate greater number of Indonesian pilgrims".
19. Rawson, Philip. *The Art of South East Asia*, London 1967. pp. 222-23.
20. Zimmer, H. *The Art of Indian Asia*, Vol. II, New York 1955, pl. 59.

9

Copper Hoard Implements in the National Museum, New Delhi : 1987 Collection

D.P. Sharma

The National Museum, New Delhi has a total of 137 Copper Hoard implements from localities of the lower and middle Ganga-Yamuna *doab* and Mehsana in Gujarat. A brief note regarding 93 implements which were acquired from 1965 to 1986 has been published earliear.[1] Present paper deals with the 42 implements which were acquired by the Museum during the year 1987.

Shri Abhinava Gupta of Allahabad brought 29 Copper Hoard implements from Kanpur, Sitapur, Shahabad (Hardoi), Lucknow and Saharanpur; all in the *doab* and these implements were purchased by us. These objects include a fragment of a lugged axe, 3 weed chisels or *khurpi*, a knife or razor, an antennae sword and 2 hooked swords. Shri Tariq Ahamad Chisti of Amroha, Moradabad, U.P sold us 13 copper implements and he alleged, that these objects were collected by him from Kanpur region. This collection includes a shouldered celt or axe, a flat celt or axe, 5 Harpoons, 2 chisels, 2 weed chisels or *khurpis*, 2 antennae swords and 2 hooked swords. Shri Pramod Puri, an art dealer from Delhi, sold us one sword and it also belongs to Kanpur-Unnao border area.

Observation

Exact find spot of any of the above objects is not known but some of them are rare.

Lugged Axe

A fragment of lugged axe from Shri Gupta collection which came from Kanpur-Unnao border is of much importance. Its elliptical working edge is intact, but two lugs and the butt end are missing. It has sharp vertical chisel marks on both the flat sides. Typologically and functionally the tool was meant to be an axe.

This is the second discovery of lugged axe in the *doab* region. Another lugged axe resembling this was reported earlier from Sitapur and is at present in the National Museum.[2] Lugged axes are also found: one from Kathmandu valley in Nepal which is now in Selmberg collection, London[3] and another from Rewari in Haryana which is now in Kanya Gurukul Museum, Narela.[4] Working edge of the lugged axe from Kathmandu valley and two of the National Museum resemble but differs from the Rewari one. When we compare the shape of Lothal authropomorph[5] with the two lugged axes of National Museum we find the lugged side of Lothal object is smaller and is similar to ours. D.P. Agrawal has some doubt about Lothal specimen, the so-called anthropomorph,[6] and the author is inclined to believe that the Lothal anthropomorph is an axe.

Shouldered Celt

There are 5 shouldered celts in this year's acquisition. Shouldered celt (Acc. No. 87.22/26) from Hardoi is very big in size. Its cutting edge is hemicircular and its end encompasses over half of its length. Sides are concave and taper in the direction of butt end. Both faces and butt end are flat. This resembles the shouldered celts from Bithur now in the Allahabad Museum.[7] Another shouldered celt (Acc. No. 87.22/27) of this year's collection from Hardoi resembles in size and shape the shouldered celt No. (Acc. No. 87.22/26)[8] acquired this year. Its edge is damaged. Third shouldered celt (No. 87.22/16) from Kanpur is a little different. Its working edge is sharp and semi-circular but it covers only one fourtn of length. Its two sides are flat and two sides taper in the direction of butt end. This resembles in shape and size the celt from Bithur in the Lucknow Museum and other one from same locality in Allahabad Museum.[9] Fourth shouldered celt (Acc. No. 87.79/11) of. Mr Tariq's collections is also from Kanpur. Its cutting edge is hemicircular and spread in one fourth of its length. Its two side edges are parallel and the end is straight and flat. Fourth celt resembles another celt of the National Museum[10] and one from Bithur now in Lucknow Museum.[11] Fifth celt (87.22/24) is a fragment and it was collected from Unnao.[12] This differs from the above four in its smaller size (11.8x12.2 cm). Its cutting edge has two concave shoulders and working edge is hemisperical and comprise over half of its length. Two concave depression on cutting edge is formed due to breakage of edge. This axe resembles the axe from Dunria, Orissa now in the Patna Museum[13] but it differs from the Bithur axe.[14]

Hooked Swords

Hooked sword (Acc. No. 87.22/2) from Shaharanpur has a prominent medial ridge and a curved hook at tang. The medial rib produces a lozenge-shaped section. Tip of the blade is semi-circular. Tang is crude, heavy and flat. The sword resembles the one sword in the National Museum of Edingburgh, U.K. and other from Niori.[15] Two such type of swords were also reported from Sarthauli and Etawah.[16]

Another Hooked sword (Acc. No. 87.22/4) from Sahabad is a little different from the above. Its blade is pointed and the medial ridge is prominant and concave. Tang is rectangular and small. This sword resembled the one of Bulandshahar, one from Saipai and two from Bahabarabad.[17] These two swords were made by mould-cast method. The hook in these swords at their tangs seems to have been intended for fastening the sword with a shaft. These swords differ from the Harappan sword without the latter hole instead of hook and are more smooth and well finished.

Antennae Swords

Antennnae sword (Acc. No. 87.22/1) from Unnao has a long broad leaf-shaped convex blade. Medial ridge of the blade is flat, thin and rectangular. Tang is short and circular. Side of the blade is damaged and covered by dark green patina. This sword resembles those from Fatehgarh,[18] Bithur, Chandausi and the one from Shahabad. Another from Kanpur (Acc. No. 87.55) is identical with the above. Its long blade is twisted and the antenne is missing. Tang is thin circular and it has two small holes. This resembles the three swords of the National Museum (Acc. No. 87.175, 67-139, and 66.28) and also one from Hissar.[19] This is made by hammer and mould method. The third (87.79/7) from Kanpur is in four pieces. Its leaf-shaped blade is long narrow and thick and tip is tilted. Medial rib is prominent and concave and made by double mould method and it shows clear traces of ancient wear. Its short round antennae are curved. This piece differs from the above two, where the antennae are comparatively longer. This resembles the sword of Moradabad, Shahabad and Fatehgarh and three from Rewari.[20] Another fragment (87.79/13) from Kanpur represents only half portion. The above four swords differ from similar swords from Mehsana; the latter has broadly furcated antennae.

Harpoons

Harpoon (87.79/5) from Kanpur has a short blade and there are three sets of barbs issuing out from the shaft occupying two thirds of length. It has two-holed lugs on the stem. It was cut from thick sheet of copper sheet and hammered into thin shape of harpoon. This resembles the one from Bithur and Shahabad.[21] Harpoon (87.22/5) of Sitapur has small short blade tip with a set of two barbs on each side. There is one hole at the lug on the stem. Midrib is developed and is half of total length. It is a fine example of craftsmanship and is cast by double mould method. This differs from above and resembles the one from Saipai and Shahabad.[22] Harpoon (87.79/4) from Kanpur is also of small short type. It has a set of three barbs on each side. It has one hole lug and a curved hook at the stem. Medial rib is prominant and is made by mould method and later on edges were trimmed. Barbs are flat on downward indentation in the shaft. It is a proto-type of bone harpoon. This Harpoon resembles the one of Nasirupr and other from Sarthauli.[23] Harpoon (87.22/3) of Hardoi is also short bladed type. It is in three pieces and three sets of barbs are arranged bilaterally. Barbs are very close to the shaft and it has also two eyelets on the two lugs. Medial rib is prominent and it is also cast by double mould method. This harpoon resembles the one of Bithur now in Lucknow Museum.[24] Harpoon (87.79/6) of Kanpur is of the longer blade type. Lance-head or blade is 2/3 of total length. Three sets of circular curved backbarbs are present. Technically and aesthetically it is of very high quality and was made by double mould method. This harpoon resembles the three from Bithur and two from Shahabad.[25] Harpoons numbered 87.79/2 and 87.79/3 both from

Kanpur are identical with the harpoon no. 87.79/6. Last three harpoons resemble the one of Bisauli, one from Hornium Museum, London, one from Berlin Museum and one from Shahabad.[26]

In all the above mentioned harpoons it was noticed the barbs are pointing back. Harpoons were used for hunting and as well as in war.

Weed Chisel or Khurpi

Weed Chisel, Tang type (87.22/17) of Shahabad is of 'V' shape. Its cutting edge is convex and side edges are straight and taper in the direction of the butt end. It has a tang near the butt end and both sides are smooth and thin. This resembles : one the tanged weed chisel from Shahabad now in the National Museum;[27] two from Bithur;[28] one from the University Museum and Archaeology and Anthropology, Cambridge;[29] and three from Rewari;[30] weed chisel was used for agricultural purpose and we have some ethnographic parallels from the *doab* region. Weed chisel (87.22/9) from Shahabad resembles the above chisel. This is also of the tanged type. These two tanged chisels were cut from thin sheet of copper and in the second stage it was hammered. Weed chisel (87.22/10) of Unnao and the remaining three are without tangs and these are rough and rectangular in shape. These chisels resemble the three weed chisels of the National Museum,[31] one from Rajpur-Parsu[32] and one from Kausambi now in British Museum, London.[33]

Chisels

Chisel (87.22/8) of Kanpur is a pointed thick weapon. It has four flat sides and the cross-section is square. Its butt end is rectangular and thick. This differs from the belt because these are smaller in size. Chisels were used for mining ores.[34] Chisel (87.79/12) of Kanpur is identical with first but the butt is of the curved type. Chisel (87.22/6) differs from above two because its working edge is wide and convex and its thickness is less than 0.5 cm. Butt end is narrow and side edges taper towards butt end. Chisel (87.22/7) of Shaharanpur and from Kanpur (87.79/1) resemble the chisel No. 87.22/6. The National Museum, New Delhi has nine more chisels in its collection.

Flat Celts

There are total ten flat celts of different shape. Flat celt (87.79/8) of Kanpur is very small. Its working edge is convex. This is rectangular in shape and is prototype of Neolithic celt of Belan Valley, Allahabad.[35] Another celt (87.22/15) of Shahabad has graffiti marks of three parallel incised lines and *trisula* figure. *Trisula* motif was also noticed on a celt of Hansi.[36] One flat axe (87.22/15) of Lucknow has incised symbol of taurine (*Nandi-Pada*).

References

1. Gupta, S.P. Copper Hoard implements in the National Museum Collection: *Puratattva* No. 16.
2. *Ibid.*
3. Yule, P. *Metal work of the Bronze Age in India*, Munich 1982, Fig. 798.
4. *Ibid.* Fig. 800
5. Rao, S.R. *Lothal and the Indus Civilisation*, London 1973.
6. Agarwal, D.P. *The Archaeology of India*, London 1982.
7. Yule, P. *op. cit.* Figure 773
8. *Ibid.* Fig. 601
9. *Ibid.* Fig. 591
10. Gupta S.P. *op. cit.* Acc No. 86.59/8
11. Shastri, H. Recent Additions to our knowledge of the Copper Age Antiquities of the Indian Empire, *J.A.S.B.* 11. 1915 pp. 1-6
12. Yule, *op. cit.* Fig. 245.
13. *Ibid.* Fig. 395.
14. *Ibid.*
15. *Ibid.* Fig. 304
16. *Ibid.* Fig. 343
17. *Ibid.* Figs. 274, 340, 234, 1043.
18. *Ibid.* Fig. 258
19. *Ibid.* Fig. 1065
20. *Ibid.* Figs. 797, 258, 1046, 1047.
21. Gt.ʾta, S.P. *op. cit.* Acc No. 85.177. and Yule, *op. cit.* Fig. 338.
22. Yule, P. *op. cit.* Fig. 338.
23. Sinha, B.C. *Marg pradarshishikar Puratattva Sangrahalaya* Hardwar, (Hindi), 1973.
24. Lal, B B. Further Copper Hoards from the Gangetic basin and a Review of the Problem, *A.I.* 7, 1951. p. 29.
25. Gordon, D.H. *The Prehistoric Background of Indian culture*, Bombay 1958.
26. Yule, *op. cit.* Figs. 1016, 1016, 1017, 1018, 1026, and 1026 and Pant, G.N. *Indian Arms and Armour*, Volume I, New Delhi. 1978.
27. Yule, *op. cit.* and Gupta S.P. *op. cit.*
28. *Ibid.*
29. *Ibid.*
30. Shastri, *op. cit.*
31. Yule, *op. cit.*
32. Gupta, *op. cit*
33. Yule, P. *op. cit.* Figur 318.
34. *Ibid.* Fig. 713.
35. Agrawal, D.P. *The Copper Bronze Age in India*, Delhi 1971.

26. Pal, J.N. *Archeology of Southern U.P.*, Allahabad 1986.
37. Yule, P. *op. cit.* Fig. 740.

The Collection : 1987

No.	Acc. No.	Description
94.	87.22/1	Antennae Sword Unnoo, U.P.
95.	87.22/2	Hooked Sword Shahabad, Hardoi 34 x 9.3 cm
96.	87.22/3	Harpoon Shahabad, Hardoi 38 x 5 cm
97.	87.22/4	Hooked Sword Shahabad, Hardoi 44 x 6.4 cm
98.	87.22/5	Harpoon Sitapur 20.5 x 4.7 cm
99.	87.22/6	Chisel Sitapur 19.6 x 2.2 cm
100.	87.22/7	Chisel Saharanpur 19.7 x 2.7 cm
101.	87.22/8	Chisel Sitapur 16.3 x 1.4 cm
102	87.22/9	Tanged chisel (*Khurpi*) Shahabad, Hardoi, 17 x 4.2 cm
103.	87.22/10	Weed chisel Unnao 16 x 11.3 cm
104.	87.22/11	Flat celt, Shahabad, Hardoi 16 x 11 cm.
105.	87.22/12	Razor Shahabad, Hardoi 16 x 11 cm
106.	87.22/13	Celt Lacknow 9.1 x 8 cm
107.	87.22/14	Lugged axe Kanpur, Unnao 8.2 x 5.7 cm
108.	87.22/15	Celt Shahabad, Hardoi 14.2 x 8.4 cm
109.	87.22/16	Shouldered celt Shahabad 14.8 x 10 cm
110.	87.22/17	Tanged Weed Chisel Shahabad, Hardoi 13.6 x 3.3 cm
111.	87.22/18	Weed Chisel Shahabad, Hardoi 21 x 7.5 cm
112.	87.22/19	Flat celt Sitapur 9 2 x 6.2 cm
113.	87.22/20	Celt (Small) Sitapur 12 x 8 cm
114.	87.22/21	Weed Chisel Sitapur 9.2 x 5.1 cm
115.	87.22/22	Celt (Small) Saharanpur 2.3 x 4.7 cm
116.	87.22/23	Celt Lucknow 9.4x6.4 cm
117.	87.22/24	Shouldered celt Unnao 11.8x12 cm
118.	87.22/25	Weed chisel Saharanpur 13x4 cm
119.	87.22/26	Shouldered celt Shahabad, Hardoi 23x18.5 cm
120.	87.22/27	Shouldered celt Shahabad Hardoi 19.4x16.5 cm
121.	87.12/28	Celt Shahabad, Hardoi 19.5x10.1 cm
122.	87.12/29	Celt Sitapur 12.5x7 cm
123.	87.79/1 a & b.	Chisel Kanpur 28x3.1 to 2.9x8 cm
124.	87.79/2	Harpoon Kanpur 31x5.5 cm
125.	87.79/3	Harpoon Kanpur 31x5 cm

126.	87.79/4	Harpoon Kanpur 30.5x7.1 cm
127.	87.79/8	Celt Kanpur 24.5x3.6 cm
128.	87.79/8	Celt Kanpur 6.3x5.1 cm
129.	87.79/7 a to d	Sword Antennae sword Kanpur 54x5x1 cm
130.	87.79/10	Weed Chisel Kanpur 25x5 cm
131.	87.79/10	Weed chisel Kanpur 17.3x5.5 cm
132.	87.79/11	Shouldered celt Kanpur 15.8x11.4 cm
133.	87.79/13	Antennae sword hilt 8.7x3.8 cm
134.	87.55	Antennae sword Kanpur 43x5.4 cm
135.	87.79/6	Harpoon Kanpur 30x5.7 cm
136.	87.79/12	Chisel Kanpur 17.5x1 cm
137.	87.79/1	Chisel Kanpur 17.7x1.3 cm

10

Buddhist Relic Caskets in Indian Museums

S.K. Bhattacharya

In the course of excavations and digging of Buddhist *stupas* in India over the several decades in the past numerous relic caskets containing relics of Buddha and other Buddhist saints were recovered and these are housed in museums and Buddhist *viharas* all over India. So far there is no authentic single publication wherein one, at a glance, could ascertain their provenance, description of the relics, etc. This is a modest attempt towards that end.

The places where these are housed are :

1. Mulagandha Kuti Vihara, Sarnath, U.P.
2. State Archaeological Museum, Patna, Bihar
3. Indian Museum, Calcutta, West Bengal
4. Dharmarajika Vihara at Calcutta, West Bengal.
5. Archaeological Museum, Nagarjunakonda, Andhra Pradesh
6. State Archaeological Museum, Egmore, Madras, Tamil Nadu
7. Archaeological Museum, Sanchi, Madhya Pradesh
8. Chetiyagiri Vihar at Sanchi, Madhya Pradesh
9. Museum of Department of Archaeology and Ancient History of M.S. University of Baroda, Vadodara.
10. Amaravati Museum, Amaravati, Andhra Pradesh
11. Asiatic Society Library, Bombay

Introduction

The Buddhist *stupas* may be grouped into four broad categories :

(i) *Saririka*, (ii) *paribhogika*, (iii) *uddesika* (memorial), and (iv) votive.

The first category, *Saririka*, signifies those erected over the corporeal relics of not only of Buddha, but also of his chief disciples as well as Buddhist teachers and saints. Throughout India reliquaries containing bones and ashes have been found enshrined in many *stupas*; but it is only in a few instances that the reliquaries bear the names of the persons concerned.

In the early *stupas*, the relic chamber was generally set either in the foundation or in the heart of the *stupa* itself. But many times relics were kept away from both the above sides in the corner of the *stupa*. The great care that was taken to preserve the sacred relics is seen in the number of caskets used, one within the other; the innermost containing the relics.

When the Viceroy announced the discovery, in Peshawar, several potative relics of the Buddha, and outlined plans for their distribution to Ceylon, Burma, China and Japan, it stimulated a great response. primarily in Bengal, among those who regarded the relics as Indian patrimony. A petition was sent to the Government from the Presidency College, Calcutta, beseeching the Government not to send the relics away to foreign lands, but to keep them in India, for they should be preserved carefully in a country, which for twenty-five long centuries has held them in her bosom.

DISPOSITION OF RELIC CASKETS AND RELICS

Dharmarajika Vihara, Calcutta

Venerable Dharmapala, a scion of a well-to-do family of Ceylon founded the Maha Bodhi Society in May 1891. During the next five years, the Dharmarajika Chaitya Vihara of the Society was built in Calcutta. The Society was presented in 1920 with a crystal casket containing the relics of the Buddha. The relics were discovered at Bhattiprolu in the Krishna district in 1891. The Dharmarajika Chaitya Vihara was formally opened on November 20, 1920.

Since the chief priest of the Vihara did not know the exact location of the casket and according to him it was probable that the casket was kept in one solid metal *stupa* which was made specially for the casket and could not be opened, no details could be obtained or photograph them.

Mulagandha Kuti Vihara, Sarnath

With the discovery of relics at Nagarjunakonda in 1921, the Viceroy offered these to the Maha Bodhi Society on condition that a suitable *stupa* should be built at Sarnath to enshrine them. For the above purpose the Mulagandha Kuti Vihara was built at Sarnath in 1931.

The relic caskets housed here are from two sites : (i) Taxila and (ii) Nagarjunakonda.

Taxila

The relics enclosed within a silver casket enshrined in the *Vihara* were found by Sir John Marshall in 1913-14 near the ancient city of Taxila (Takshasila), now in Pakistan, in a small Buddhist chapel close to the Dharmarajika Stupa. It was found near the back wall of the chapel opposite the great Stupa and about 30 cm below the original floor. It consists of vase-shaped casket of grey micaceous schist with a silver vase inside. In the latter an inscribed scroll of silver and a small gold casket containing some minute bone pieces were found.[1] This incription which is in the Kharoshthi character and dated in the year 136 of Azes (*c*. A.D. 78) tells us that the relics were those of the Lord Buddha. The incription reads :

"In the year 136 of Azes, on the 15th day of the Holy One (Buddha) were enshrined by Urasaka, scion of Cintavkria, a Bactrian, resident of the town Naocha."

Nagarjunakonda

These relics found by Mr A.H. Longhurst in 1929 in a large stupa at Nagarjunakonda, within the Mahachaitya in one of the outermost north-western cells, was believed to have been that of Buddha, on the basis of an incription found at the site. The present silver casket is a modern replica of the original casket, which was found in broken condition. Originally it was placed in gold reliquary, the latter with a few gold flowers, pearls and pieces of garnet and crystal kept inside a silver *stupa*-shaped casket. The silver casket in its turn with three large crystal and an ear stud was deposited in an earthen pot.

After opening the casket by Venerable Dodamgoda Rawatha Thero, High priest of the *Vihara* it was found difficult to make out the distinction between the two relics. Only one piecc of bone and some ash-like substance are kept in one small inverted glass, which was again kept in one modern casket, presented by one Burmese a few years ago.

The High Priest informed me that about twenty years ago most of the things were stolen away from the Vihara. The Maha Bodhi Society at Sarnath has no record of the stolen things.

Relic casket from Vaisali, State Archaeological Museum, Patna

In one of the breaches in the *stupa* the reliccasket was found lying by itself without any enclosing stone box. The casket had cracked due to the heavy pressure of earth lying directly above it. The relic casket is made of some soft stone, most likely steatite.

The casket contained no bone relic, but only ashes mixed with earth. Along with these relics there were punch-marked copper coin, two glass beads, one conch and a thin small piece of gold.[2]

The Patna Museum records show these as :

One steatite[3] Relic casket containing ashes, one broken conch and a thin tiny piece of gold.

Size : Height 5.4 cm
Diameter : 4.5 cm
This casket is dated to the pre-Mauryan period.

However neither the beads nor the punch-marked coin is found mentioned.

Relic Casket from Piprahwa, Dist. Basti (U.P.), now in Indian Museum, Calcutta

Piprahwa, had one of the largest *stupas* so far found in India and it was exposed by W.C. Peppe in the year 1897.[4] The following things were found in the excavation, and all of them are now in the Indian Museum, Calcutta.

1. Stone Coffer, 1.33 m long at the base, 65 cm wide at the base and 63 cm in height (together with the fitting lid) was 1.30 x 65x 63 cm and was found broken in four pieces. The lid had four roughly semi-circular projections, two each on the longer sides, for easy lifting.

Inside it were found; (i) a steatite vase, 19 cm high and 11.5 cm in maximum diameter; (ii) a similar but inscribed vase of the same material, 14.5 cm high and 11.5 cm in diameter; (iii) a steatite *lota*-shaped vessel, 13.5 cm high (without lid) and 13.5 cm in maximum diameter, (iv) a round casket, also of steatite, 8.5 cm in maximum diameter and 5 cm high; and; (v) an exquisitely polished crystal casket, 11.5 cm in maximum diameter and 10.5 cm high (together with its cover). The handle of the last was in the shape of a hollow fish stuffed with seven gold bands having gold granulated six-petalled flowers and gold circular frames attached to them and several tiny beads in paste. Besides these, there were wooden and silver vessels which had been reduced to pieces. The contents of these vases were both rich and varied and included, apart from pieces of bone, gold leaves impressed with various symbols like *svastika*, *triratnas*, triangle-headed standard, etc., impressions of two female figures on gold leaf, figures of animals like lion and elephant in gold leaf, gold and silver flowers and stars, a tiny amulet-like gold box, *triratnas*, a gold disc impressed with profusely connected spirals, plain gold bars, rolls of gold leaves numerous pearls, with or without perforations, a carnelian bird, a malachite bird, delicately fashioned leaves, *seed* vessels, *triratnas*, and flowers in semi-precious stones, fragment of coral, beads of various shapes in gold, silver, semi-precious stones, pieces of mica and a spiral of copper wire-perhaps a ring.

The most important is the inscription on the lid of the smaller steatite vase. Some scholars have interpreted that the relics are those of Buddha himself. While some others opine that they were of Buddha's kinsmen and their sisters' wives and children[5] who were killed by Vidudabha.

A pre-Asokan date has been assigned for the inscription in view of the absence of the signs for long medial vowels, though the characters are similar to those of the edicts of Asoka.[6]

In the well known *stupa* in which the inscribed relic casket was found, a trench was laid towards the western end in 1972 by the Archaeological Survey of India to ascertain the number of stages in which it was built. At a depth of six metres from the top, two burnt brick chambers were found in the centre. When three courses of bricks were removed, the pinnacle of a soapstone casket came to light. The maximum diameter of the casket was 7 cm and the height 12 cm. It contained charred bones. When two further courses of bricks were removed another soapstone casket with its lid broken in three pieces was sighted. This soapstone casket was bigger in size, the maximum diameter being 9 cm and height 16 cm. Like the other casket this was also packed perfectly between bricks and brickbats. Charred bones were found inside the casket. The caskets are of two parts, the body as the container with a broad base, and a lid to fit closely on the top. Both these caskets are now displayed in The National Museum, New Delhi.

Caskets could be dated to 5th-4th century B.C. i.e. earlier in date than the inscribed relic casket discovered by Peppe at a higher level in 1898.[7]

Nagarjunakonda, Andhra Pradesh

During the excavation of the important *stupas* of Nagarjunakonda (Nos. 1, 3, 4, 5, 6 and 8 of Longhurst,[8] stupa 9 and 21) yielded reliquaries of gold, silver, copper and glazed pottery.

The relic casket which was found in the Mahachaitya was believed to have been that of Buddha. It was placed in a gold reliquary, the latter with a few gold flowers, pearls and pieces of garnet and crystal kept inside a silver casket with three large crystal beads and an ear stud and was deposited in an earthen pot. More meticulous care was noticed in *stupa* 8 of Longhurst, when the bone relics was preserved in a series of *stupa*-shaped caskets, one within the other; the innermost one being of gold, the next silver the third of copper, the next of earthenware and the outermost of stone. The other objects which were found in the gold casket are silver flowers, gold flowers, three gold balls, gold leaf with lotus flowers and a bone piece.

There were some more caskets which were excavated from different *stupas* at Nagarjunakonda. Some of them are in a very fragile condition. They are from the following *stupas* :

Stupa No. 2

1. Acc. No. 439: Silver caskets in fragments, 3rd-4th Cent. A.D.
2. Acc. No. 440: Gold casket, damaged.

Stupa No. 3

1. Acc. No. 448: Fragment of copper casket.

2. Acc. No. 449: Gold Relic casket (mentioned by Longhurst as that casket of silver)
3. Acc. No. 450: Gold casket.

Stupa No. 4

1. Acc. No. 459: Fragment of a silver casket.
2. Acc. No. 460: Stupa-shaped gold casket.

Stupa No. 6

1. Acc. No. 472 : Gold casket.
2. Acc. No. 475 : Fragment of a silver caket.

Relic Caskets from Battiprolu in Andhra Pradesh, Govt. Museum, Madras

In 1892 Alexander Rea made partial excavation of the *stupa*, which was built of solid bricks. The most outstanding discovery of Rea was three inscribed receptacles found in the centre of the *stupa* and which were placed at different levels near the foundation of the stupa.

First Casket

A large irregular three-sided slab of black stone was found embedded in the brick on the south side of the *stupa*. It measures about 76 x 66 x 17 cm. It seems to be the lid of the large stone casket. Its under surface is smoothed (actually polished) and has a rectangular cutting, measuring 26 x 20 x 1 cm deep. It lay on the top of another similar but thicker stone which formed the receptacle for a number of relics. Its size is 69 x 56 x 33 cm. On the upper surface is a cavity 11.5 cm deep, and circular at the bottom, but sloping up to a rectangular top with raised rim made to fit into the hollow in the lid. The upper surface of the stone is smooth (plished), and inscribed in a new type of the southern Mauryan Character.[9] In the cavity there was a black stone relic casket. Around this casket and mixed with the earth which filled the cavity were the following articles: Copper ring and several bits of copper, a small bead and two double pearls, two small semi-spherical cups made of hard brown metal. On the apex of the lid is a bead. An hexagonal crystal head 6 5 cm long with slightly convex sides, pierced with a hole was also found here. On each of the sides there is inscription in a character similar to that on the stone.

There were two *trisula*-like objects made of thin sheets of pure gold and four flowers with eight petals. There was also a hollow single and double gold bead and seven small triangular flowers of gold.

Inside the the globular casket and lying below the crystal phial were nine small flowers of various sizes in gold leaf and gold beads, nineteen small pierced pearls and a slighty blue coloured amethyst bead. Fixed on the bottom by oxidation and arranged in the form of a svastika were twenty-four small silver coins.

Second Casket

Below the above casket another black stone was found. It was the lid, and another stone which lay below it, was the receptacle of a second relic casket. The covering stone is roughly triangular in form with rounded corners, and measures 68 x 63 x 25 cm. On the top is a circle 18.5 cm in diameter, raised on one centimetre above the surface. The underside is smooth and has a circular space 1 cm deep and 30 cm in diameter. In this circle is an inscription in ninteen lines, while around it is another in two lines. The stone receptacle is roughly rectangular with round corners and measures 50 x 44 x 30 cm. On the upper surface is a circular hole 16 cm deep, 18 cm in diameter at the top and 10 cm at the bottom. Around the top is a raised rim 3 cm broad, which fits into the hollow lid. Around and outside the rim is an inscription in two lines. There is no inner stone casket as in the first. It was a crystal phial. Its lid is just like a *stupa*. The hollow in the vessel is cylindrical. The following articles were found: 164 gold flowers of varying sizes; they have six, eight and nine petals and some were fitted inside each other with a gold bead as a bud. Two circular flowers, a two-armed figure were also noticed. In these are in gold leaf or thin sheet of gold six hollow gold beads, and a small coiled gold ring, two pearls, a garnet, six coral beads, a slightly blue flat oval crystal bead and a pointed oval white crystal bead. There were a number of bits of corroded copper leaf, including flowers and stems, and a miniature umbrella.

Third Casket

The third and the last casket was found lying on the east side of the *stupa*. The lid is an irregular circular stone measuring about 72 x 63 x 24 cm. On its surface is a circular space sunk 1 cm, having an inscription in eight lines. The stone receptacle which it covered is roughly square in shape and measures 74 x 68 x 28 cm. On the upper surface is a circular cavity 14 cm deep, 18 cm in its upper diameter and 12 cm at the bottom. Around it is a rim, which fits into the hollow in the lid. Outside of the rim is a circular inscription in one line. In the cavity there was a crystal phial similar in shape that found in the second casket, but slightly larger. Close to the phial lay minature relic casket made of a beryl. There are three small pieces of bone. The beryl casket was the phial. A cylindrical hole is drilled in its axis in which are the relics. The hole is closed by a small white crystal stopper with hexagonal top, with a sheet of gold leaf fixed on it. A loose sheet of gold closes the joint at the neck and another is placed outside on the bottom. The following other things are found along with the phial: two amethyst beads, a yellow crystal bead, six pearls and thirty-two pearl beads, thirty flowers, a bent two-armed figure, and a small foil in gold leaf. Few bits of copper are also found.[10]

The inscription records the names of a large number of individuals, belonging to different families and guilds, and a king called Kabesaka, who earned merit by sharing in the donation of the contents of the receptacles. It is however, not known whether the same individuals contributed towards the raising of the *stupa* as well. The inscriptions have been dated by some scholars to about 200 B.C. or slighly earlier.[11]

Relic Caskets from Amaravati Stupa, Andhra Pradesh

Amaravati, on the right bank of the Krishna river, had the biggest *stupa* in Andhra Pradesh, and the same has been mentioned in an inscription of 2nd century A.D. as *Mahachaitya*. Five reliccaskets, made of rock-crystal, were recovered recently from the base slab of the *ayaka* pillars of the southern *ayaka* platform. The four caskets are in the shape of a *stupa* and the fifth cylindrical. Inside the caskets were lodged bones and gold flowers.[12]

Relics caskets from Sanchi

All the *stupas* at Sanchi and near about Sanchi have yielded relic caskets. Though none of them belong to Buddha, the inscriptions found on them clearly and definitely mention that they are relics of the disciples of Buddha.

All these relic caskets were taken away to the British Museum, London; only the plaster casts are available in the Sanchi Archaeological Museum, which were prepared in 1956. The relics and replicas of two caskets of Sariputra and Maha Mogallana were presented to Maha Bodhi Society for enshrinement in the Chetiyageri Vihara at Sanchi and they are taken out once in a year on the occasion of Buddha Purnima.

Stupà No. 1 at Sanchi

Two pieces, which were supposed to be of an umbrella, are actually the lid of a massive stone relic coffer which stood, crowned by an umbrella on the top of the *stupa*. It was this relic coffer no doubt, which Captain Fell saw in 1819 and he described it as being split in pieces. It is of local variety yellow sandstone, concave on the underside and provided with a rim around its under edge, and with a square mortise on the top. into which the umbrella shaft (*yashti*) was presumably inserted. This relic coffer, which is not of Maurya workmanship was no doubt contempoary with the outer stone of the drum. What relics it contained can only be surmised but it seems likely that any relic other than those of the Buddha himself would have been preserved in so important a monument.[13]

Stupa No. 2 at Sanchi

This *stupa* was first opened by Cap. Johnson in 1822, but it was Gen. Cunningham who found the casket in 1851. The chamber in which the relics were deposited was in the centre of the *stupa*. The casket was of white sandstone measuring 24 x 21 cm. It contained four small caskets of steatite. in each of which were some fragments of human bones. One of the sides, of the relic box was an inscription in early Brahmi characters mentioning that it contained the relics "of all teachers including Kasapagota and vachi-Suvijayita.[14] On the four steatite caskets were other inscriptions giving the names of the ten saints whose relics were in the caskets, some of whom are said to have taken part in the Third Council under the aegis of Asoka, while others were sent out on missions to the Himalayas to preach the doctorine. These two saints are as follows: Kasapagota, the teacher of the Thamavatas Majjhima, Haritiputa, Vachi-Suvijayita, pupil of Gota, Mahavanaya, Apagira Kodineputa, Kosikiputa, Gotiputa, and Mogaliputta.

Stupa No. 3 at Sanchi

The relic chamber, in which the relics were found intact by General Cunningham, was set up in the centre of the dome of *stupa*. Covering it was a large slab and inside were two stone boxes, each with a a single name inscribed in early Brahmi characters on the lid. On the top of the south was Sariputra, and on the north, Mahamogatanasa. The lids measures 61 x 57 x 14 and 51 x 30 x 11 cm. respectively.

In Sariputra's box was a flat casket of white steatite. It has been turned on a lathe and its surface is hard and polished. The size of the casket is 15 cm long and 8 cm. in height. The casket was covered by a thin saucer of black lustrous earthen ware. Close to the steatite casket were two pieces of sandalwood.

Within the casket was a small fragment of bone and several beads of pearl, garnet, lapis-lazuli, crystal and amethyst. Inside the lid was written the letter *'sa'*, no doubt the initial of 'Sariputa'.

In Mahamogatana's box was a second casket of steatite, smaller than Sariputra's, which has the letter *'Ma'*, and contained two small fragments of bones only.

Stupa No. 2 at Sonari, M P.

A large steatite vase was profusely but coarsely ornamented with elephants and horses. Inside this vase were found five relic caskets each containing human bones with an inscription recording the name of the person whose relics were enshrined therein.

Casket No. 1

It is a round flat box of crystal, 15 cm in height and 5 cm in diameter. As the crystal was too hard to be inscribed, the name and title of the holy man was carved on a small piece of stone. The inscription, which is engraved on both sides, is one of the most interesting discoveries and mentions "(Relics) of the emancipated Gotiputra", the brother of religion amongst the Dardabhisoras of the Hemawanta.'

Casket No. 2

The casket is of dark mottled steatite, hemi spherical in shape, with a flat bottom and pinnacled top. The inscription is engraved on the outside of the lid. It mentions that the casket contained "(Relics) of the emancipated Majhsma the son of Kodini".

Casket No. 3

It is also of a dark mottled steatite, nearly hemispherical in shape, with a flat bottom and pinnacled top. The inscription, engraved around the outside of the lid mentions: "(Relics) of the emancipated son of Koti, Kasyapa Gotra, the missionary to the whole Hemawanta".

Casket No. 4

It is similar to Nos 2 and 3. The inscription engraved on the top at the lid mentions "(Relics) of the emancipated Kosikiputra".

Casket No. 5

It is made of black steatite and is shaped somewhat like a pear and the outside is ornamented by a succession of traingles, alternately plain and crossed. The inscription occupies the plain triangles on the lower half of the casket.

The erection of this *stupa*, which contained the relics of no less than four of the Buddhist teachers whose ashes had already been discovered in the stupa No. 2 at Sanchi, must evidently belong to the same period, i.e. towards the end of the third century B.C.

Stupa No. 2 Satadhara, M.P.

Two small steatite caskets containing bones. were found at the bottom of the *stupa*. These caskets are of pale mottled steatite, each 8 cm in diameter and 5 cm in height. There is an inscription inside each lid; one with 'Sariputa" (Relics of Sariputra), and the other with "*Maha-Mogatanas*" (Relics of Mogatana).

Stupa No. 2 Andher, M.P.

Here a large box of red earthenwere measuring 23 cm in diameter and 19 cm in height, was found inside a chamber. The earthen pot has a small flat casket of red earthen ware and a tall steatite casket; both inscribed. There is another large steatite vase with the neck slightly broken with complete inscription.

The flat earthenware casket in 8 cm. in diameter, and nearly 3.5 cm in height. The inscription on the outside is partially obliterated but for a few letters, the sense is easily gathered and purposes to contain "(Relics) of the emancipated Vachhiputra (son of Vachhi), the pupil of Goti-putra".

The relics of Vachhi himself were found in Stupa No. 2 at Sanchi.

The tall steatite casket is 9 cm. in diameter at bottom and 5.5 cm. at the top, with a height of 14 cm. It is ornamented on the outside by bands of moulding, between which the whole surface is divided into triangles, alternately plain and barred. The insciption on the top of the lid mentions that "Relics of the emancipated son of Goti, Kakanava, Prabhasana of the race of Kodial for Kohludinva".

The large steatite vase is made in two pieces, which were fastened together with lac. It is ornamented with elephants, horses and some other winged animals of crude execution, and have a narrow neck, without lid, and was once provided with a spout; only a hole remaining now. On the upper rim of the neck there is the following inscription meaning: "(Relics) of the emancipated Mogaliputra, the pupil of Gotiputra".[11]

8. Relic, Casket from Devnimori Gujarat

The Department of Archaeology and Ancient Indian History, M.S. University, Baroda conducted excavations at Devinimori from 1960-63. This excavation yielded Buddha's relic casket which clearly mentions that these are the relics of Dashabala (Buddha). Here from the Mahastupa two caskets were obtained. Both of them were in an earthen pot.

Casket No. 1

This casket is made of schist. It is cylindrical, and measures 12 cm high and 1.8 cm thick at the top. It is an unfinished casket showing chisel marks on the interior and exterior. Its lid was better finished. This casket contains only ashes. The lid was found in fragments.

Casket No. 2

This casket is more interesting, it is made in three pieces.

1. Knob on the lid; 2. The lid; and 3. The body.

The knob is round at the top, but the lower portion is square. This square projection fits perfectly in the hole perforated in the centre of the lid.

The lid is circular and is made to fit on the body of the casket. The body is also turned on lathe. At its centre was a small pivot which was broken after the casket was made. The body is also cylindrical. On the rim there is a ledge on which the lid was correctly fitted. This casket is inscribed. The gold, silver, foil and other material were placed in it.

Inside this casket was a cylindrical copper box with flat top and bottom. In it silk bags, gold bottle and some organic material were placed. The small amphora like gold bottle has a saggar base, cylindrical body and narrow neck. Its lid is of the screw type. It was found lying loose in the copper box. The entire round surface along with the lid is inscribed in the Brahmi script that was prevalent in western India during the 4th-5th century A.D.

Sopara Caskets

Sopara (Modern Nala Sopara) has been identified with ancient Surparaka or Soparaka mentioned in the *Mahavamsa, Divyavadana, Mahabharata, Sripalacharita* and other Buddhist, Brahmanical and Jaina texts, and in the inscriptions of the Western Indian caves.

Here in 1882 Pandit Bhagvan Lal Indiraji excavated in the centre of the *stupa* and discovered a relic casket about 20 cm. from the top. Within this he found in *situ* the eight metal images representing the Seven Buddhas, and Maitreya the Future Buddha, seated aruond a copper casket, which in turn encased within in it four other caskets, placed one within the other, viz. silver, jade, crystal and finally gold. The gold casket contained thirteen tiny pieces of earthenware. There were several gold flowers in each casket and a gold plaque depicting a seated Buddha and a silver coin of Gautamiputra Yajna Sri Satakarni (*circa* A.D. 174—203) in the copper casket. All these are now in the collection of the Asiatic Society of Bombay.[16]

References

1. Marshall, J. *Taxila*, Cambridge 1951, Vol. I, pp. 256-57; Vol. III, Pl. 53C.
2. Sinha, B.P. and Roy, S.R. *Vaisali Excavations (1958-1962)*, Patna 1969, pp. 21-22, Pl. VIII.
3. Mitra, D. *Buddhist Monuments*, Calcutta 1971, pp. 75. She mentions that it is made of soapstone.
4. Peppe, W.C. The Piprahwa Stupa, containing relics of *Journal of the Royal Asiatic Society of Great Britain and Ireland*, 1898, pp. 573-78.
5. Srivastava, K.M. New Light on the Piprahwa Vase inscription, *Studies in Indian Epigraphy*, Vol. II, pp. 100-110.
6. Mitra, D. *op. cit*. pp. 80.
7. Srivastava, K.M. *Buddha's Relics From Kapilvastu*, Delhi 1986, pp. 35-37.
8. Longhurst, A.H. Excavations at Nagarjunakonda, *Annual Report*, A.S.I , 1927-28, Calcutta 1931, pp. 113-21.
9. Buhler, G. A New Variety of the Southern Maurya Alphabet, *Journal of the Royal Asiatic Society*, 1982 pp. 602-9.
10. Rea, Alexander. *South Indian Buddhist Art and Antiquities*, Madras 1894, pp. 9-12.
11. *Ep. Ind.*, II, pp. 323ff; Sircar, D.C. *Select Inscriptions*, Vol. I, Calcutta 1965, pp. 224-225, fn. 5.
12. *Indian Archaeology 1958-59—A Review*, pp. 5, Pl. II A.; Sarkar, H. *Amaravati*, New Delhi 1972, pp. 9, 28.
13. Marshall, Sir John, *Monuments of Sanchi*, Vol. I, pp. 32 and Vol. II, Pl. IV.
14. Luders List of Brahmi Inscriptions, *Ep. Ind.*, Vol. X, No. 654.
15. Cunningham, A. *The Bhilsa Topes or Monuments of Central India*, London 1854, Reprint, Varanasi 1966, pp. 225.
16. Desai, Devangana, Sopara-Pandit Bhagvan Lal Indraji and After, *Journal of the Asiatic Society of Bombay*, Vols. 56, 59, 1986, pp. 7-8 Pl. I b.

11

Technical Examination of Some Medieval Glazed Wares from Fatehpur Sikri

O.P. Agrawal, Kamal K. Jain and Tej Singh

Introduction

Fatehpur Sikri situated at 27° 5'N and 77° 40'E, and about 36 km west of Agra in Northern India was developed to be a principal city of the Moghul Empire during the 16th century, though some structures of Fatehpur Sikri complex are quite early.

A large scale development of Fatehpur Sikri was ordered during Babur's regime in 1527, and at that time some structures were constructed. The principal buildings of the great palace of Fatehpur Sikri were built by the Moghul Emperor Akbar. The city complex was completed by 1577 in less than a decade's time. But, unfortunately, Akbar had to leave Fatehpur Sikri in 1585, and soon after several buildings started collapsing for want of proper maintenance, and by 1610 the whole city was lying like a waste desert and large parts of the palace were in ruins.[1]

The records of the history of the palace buildings after Jahangir's reign are extremely scanty. At the end of the last century, E.W. Smith made his monumental survey in the 1890s,[2] although much changes have taken place at the hands of man and time since then. Therefore, almost every building outside the main palace and the mosque needed scientific excavation and study, to understand the city complex of Fatehpur Sikri in its proper perspective.

The Archaeological Survey of India in collaboration with the Centre of Advanced Studies, Department of History, Aligarh Muslim University, Aligarh has undertaken excavation of Fatehpur Sikri complex. Many building structures, hitherto buried under soil, have been exposed and a wide variety of ceramics, glass and other objects have been excavated. The ceramic objects included porcelain imported from China, glazed terracotta and ceramic ware pieces (probably of bowls) appearing as faience. Any evidence of faience industry existing in the region in the 16th century is not available. The faience objects found at Fatehpur Sikri could be of local manufacture, if any faience industry existed then, or imported from Near-East countries where faience industry was in existance since thousands of years.

Therefore, with a view to understand the technique of manufacturing and the probable origin of the glazed wares excavated at Fatehpur Sikri, investigations on some representative objects obtained from the centre of Advanced Studies, Department of History, Aligarh Muslim University were carried out and the results on the studies are presented in this paper.

EXPERIMENTAL

Equipment

A large Quartz Emission spectrograph (Higher and Watts, U.K.) was used for the qualitative analysis of the samples.

For quantitative estimation of minor elements, an Atomic Absorption Spectrometer (Perkin-Elmer, USA; Model 2380) was used.

A Philips PW 1390 X-ray Generator was used for X-ray diffraction studies for the identification of crystalline phases.

Description of the Objects

The objects selected for the studies are briefly described in Table 1. The object C as a representative of the objects is shown in Pl. 1.

Samples

The core material and the glazes of different colours were taken separately for analysis. Details of the samples are given in Table 2.

Sample Decomposition Procedure

Approximately 20 mg of accurately weighed sample was taken in a High Pressure Teflon Bomb (Uniseal Decomposition Vessels Ltd., Israel). The sample was wetted with 5 drops of aqua-regia and then 1 ml of hydrofluoric acid (40%) was added to it. The bomb was tightly closed and kept for 30 min. in an oven maintained at 110±2°C. The bomb was allowed to cool and opened. 15 ml of warm aqueous 60% solution of boric acid (JMC 330 specpure, Johnson Matthey, U.K.) was added to it and the solution was diluted to 25 ml in a volumetric flask. The solution was stored in a polythene bottle. All the samples were treated in the same manner. A blank was also prepared similarly.

Standards for atomic absorption measurements contained similar concentrations of hydrofluoric acid and boric acid.

Elemental Analysis

The samples were first analysed qualitatively for the element present by emission spectrography using a d.c. arc for excitation. Powdered samples were mixed with spectroscopic grade graphite powder and arced in graphite cup electrodes using counter electrodes of graphite rods from Ultra Carbon Corporation, U.S.A.

Quantitative analyses for calcium, copper, iron, magnesium and manganese were done by atomic absorption spectrophotometry using an air-acetylene flame and single element hollow cathode lamps. Determinations for potassium and sodium were done in emission mode, using an air-acetylene flame.

Silica content of the samples was determined gravimetrically.

X-Ray Diffraction Studies

Crystalline phases in the samples were identified by x-ray diffration technique with powder diffraction method using Debye-Scherrer camera of 114.5 mm diameter and Cu-K∝ radiations. The X-ray tube was operated at 45 KV and 35 mA. The exposure time was 8 hrs.

RESULTS AND DISCUSSION

Results on the elemental composition of the samples expressed in percentage as oxides, alongwith the elements detected but not quantified, are given in Table 2.

Main constituent of the core-samples of the objects A and B is silica, alongwith minor and trace impurities of iron etc. Core of the object B is not perfectly white and this can be attributed to its iron content. Object C which is having greyish-red core, had moderately high concentration of iron. Alkali contents of the core samples of the objects A and B were significantly low. Silica in absence of alkalies requires high temperature for vitrification. Very loosely held partiles of the cores of A and B suggest that high temperatures were not used for the firing of these objects. Core of the object C had small percentage of alkalies. This might have resulted in its partial incipient vitrification which imparted strength to the core. Crystalline phase in the core samples, as identified by the X-ray diffraction studies, was found to be ∝-quartz, associated with very small amounts of tridymite, another crystalline form of silica. At temperatures above 867°C, SiO_4^{-4} tetrahedra of ∝-quartz are torn apart and rearranged in tridymite form.[3] Though, this transformation is sluggish, significant amounts of tridymite would have formed, had the firing temperature of these objects been much higher than 867°C. In all likelihood, a temperature of approximately, 900°C, sufficient to form glass/glaze, seems to have been reported for similar objects.[4]

The glaze is soda-type, with significant impurities of aluminium (Based on qualitative measurements) and can be characterised by low alkali content. Deep blue colour in glazes is because of cobalt and the bluish green colour due to copper. Presence of tin in bluish green colour suggests that possibly bronze powder or corrosion product of bronze had been used as the colouring material.

Microscopic Examination

Particles of the core material when viewed under magnification appeared angular, and of very irregular shapes. Size of the grains varied over a wide range from about 20 um to 400 um, suggesting that the material of the core was crushed rock/stone. The core material was identified by X-ray diffraction to be mainly quartz, indicating that the white core of objects A and B was made of powdered white quartz pebbles and that of the objects C of powdered stone, may be ferruginous siliceous rock.

The glazed layer was fairly uniform in thickness, ranging between 200-300 um with an average of approximately, 250 um. These measurements were done on coloured portions of glazes. White glaze appeared colourless on magnification, therefore, it was difficult to measure thickness of white portions of glazes, although it appeared to be of similar thickness as the coloured portions.

The decorative designs on these objects, with blue or bluish green colour on a white background, could not have been produced by any of the three techniques described by Tite *et al.*[5], or by single stage application of the glazing mixture. The glaze material and the colouring material were possibly applied in two stages. The colour of the designs, when viewed under magnification, appeared dispersed in the glaze. This suggests that application of the colouring material was done after glazing mixture had been applied on the objects, followed by a single stage firing. The colouring material was most probably not applied in a solid form, since in the solid form the colouring material could not have penetrated in the glaze layer. The bluish green colouring material must have necessrrily been taken in a colloidal suspension form because it would have been difficult to have Cu-Sn in solution. In all likelyhood, cobalt must have also been applied as colloidal suspension.

The glaze layer under microscope was seen to contain numerous tiny air bubbles distributed throughout the layer. This could happen if the glazing material consisted of carbonates/bicarbonate/nitrates and not very high temperatures were used fcr firing. The molten glaze layer was not having enough fluidity to allow the escape of the carbondioxide or other gas bubbles, formed as a result of the decomposition of the carbonates/bicarbonates/nitrates. These gas bubbles could also be formed if gum had been used as binding material for shaping the body of the objects, as is the practice in Iran to use Gum Tragacanth dissolved in water to shape beads of finely ground quartzite.[6]

Conclusion

White core of the objects A and B was made with crushed white quartz pebbles, whereas, powdered ferruginous siliceous rock was, possibly, used for making the core of the object C. The glaze material was soda paste having considerable impurities of iron and, may be aluminium also. Deep blue colour was produced by cobalt and for bluish green colour, bronze or its corrosion product, in the form of a colloidal suspension, might have been used. The glazing material was applied as paste after the object had been shaped followed by application of the colouring material and then firing the objects at approximately 900°C.

The object C is different from object A and B in many respects and could have different origin.

Acknowledgement

The authors are thankful to Professor R.C. Gaur, Director, Centre for Advanced Studies, Department of History, Aligarh Muslim Unviersity for providing the objects studied and Shri Hari Narain and Shri D.G. Suryawanshi of N.R.L.C. for their help in microscopic examinations.

References

1. Rizvi S.A. and Flynn V.J. *Fatehpur Sikri*, Taraporevala, Bombay 1957, p. 14.

2. Smith E.W. *The Moghul Architecture of Fatehpur Sikri*, Parts I-IV, A S.I, New Imperial Series, XVIII, Allahabad 1894-98

3. Bailor J.C. Emeleus H.J. Nyholm R. and Trotman-Dickenson, A.F. (Eds.) *Comprehensive Inorganic Chemistry*, Pergamon Press, Oxford 1, 1973, p. 1390.

4. Goffor, Z. *Archeaological* [*Chemistry*, Wiley-Interscience, New York, 1980, p. 123.

5. Tite, M.S. Freestone, I.C. and Bimson, M. Egyptian Faince: An Investigation of the Methods of Production, *Archaeometry*, 25 (1), 1983, pp. 17-27

6. *Ibid.*

TABLE 1. DESCRIPTION OF THE OBJECTS

Object	Identification	Core	Glaze
A	FPS—I ZF_2 (2) 50 cm Thickness; 7 mm—15 mm Base of a bowl ?	Very weak and highly porous white body. Body material particles very loosely held together.	Design with blue on white on both sides.
B	FPS—I ZF_2 (2) 50 cm Thickness 4 mm—7 mm side piece of a bowl ?	Weak and porous white body. Body material particles loosely held together.	Design with deep blue on white on both sides.
C	FPS—I D_3 (2) 20 cm Thickness 8 mm—13 mm Base of a bowl ?	Highly porous, greyish red but not very weak body.	Design with bluish green on white inner side. No design on outer side.

TABLE 2. COMPOSITION OF SAMPLES

NRLC Sample No.	Description	Concentration (%)								Element present but not quantified*
		SiO_2	Na_2O	K_2O	CaO	MgO	MnO	Fe_2O_3	CuO	
47	Blue Glaze of Object A	60.0	9.2	2.0	3.0	0.5	0.05	1.2	<0.05	Co
48	White Glaze of Object A	70.0	5.9	1.7	0.6	0.5	0.04	0.8	<0.05	
49	Core (White) of Object A	97.3	<0.1	<0.1	0.3	<0.1	<0.01	0.1	<0.05	
50	Dark Blue Glaze of Object B	71.4	5.5	1.0	0.2	0.2	0.02	0.9	0.11	Co
51	Core (White) of Object B	96.3	<0.1	<0.1	0.2	<0.1	<0.01	0.3	<0.05	
52	Bluish Green Glaze of Object C	79.3	4.5	0.9	0.1	0.2	0.03	0.7	1.12	Sn
53	Core (greyish red) of Object C	90.2	0.6	0.5	0.1	<0.1	0.03	1.0	0.19	
54	White glaze of Object C	77.5	5.4	1.0	<0.1	0.2	0.02	0.9	<0·05	

*Al, B and Ti were present in all glaze samples in varying amounts.

NOTES AND NEWS

12

Stone Age Research in Keonjhar District, Orissa

Pradeep Mohanty

Archaeological explorations as part of Stone Age studies of the district have, over the last five years, brought to light fifty-seven Mesolithic sites for the first time in Keonjhar. These sites are distributed over the Champua, Ghasipura, Ghatagaon, Palaspal and Patana taluks of the district.

Most of these sites are associated with granitic outcrops, while a few are found in the foothill region lying close to streams. The artefactual spreads at individual sites vary widely; the largest ones measure approximately 20,000 square metres in extent, but intermediate ones measure around 2,500 sqare metres and the smallest can be only 100 square metres. Most of the sites are now located in dense forests.

The majority of sites discovered are primary in nature and still preserve habitational deposits. The occurrence of isolated Mesolithic artefacts in association with rock outcrops was also observed at quite a few places. Altough these occurrences may not be called "sites" in the conventional sense, their significance for interpreting the Mesolithic cultural system cannot be entirely ignored.

A well developed blade technology is the most outstanding feature of the microlithic assemblages. Chert is the principal raw material, followed by quartz, chalcedony and lydianite. The lithic component is characterised by backed-blades, obliquely truncated blades, retouched blades, burins, knives, triangles, trapezes, crescents, lunates, side-scrapers, round scrapers, steep scrapers, thumbnail scrapers, flake cores, blade cores, micro-blade-cores, utilized blades, flakes and chips.

However, the most outstanding feature of these assemblages is the occurrence of heavy duty implements made of different raw materials, chiefly dolerite, followed by quartzite, and limestone. In most of the sites heavy implements and microlithic artefacts co-occur in mixed clusters.

The heavy-duty implements comprise choppers, chopping tools, horsehoof scrapers, picks, knives, large scrapers, limaces and flakes. Celts fashioned by means of flaking, pecking, grinding and polishing, are another interesting category of implement.

The horsehoof scraper is predominant among these heavy duty implements. In general, these have steep edges are obtained by means of step-flaking. These artefacts are mostly made on thick doleritic slabs and nodules. Most were prepared by minimum flaking along their margins, leaving much cortex intact. In all cases the flat bottom of the raw material has been retained. Flake scars are generally shallow and do not show any prior preparation of the core. The nature of the flaking suggests use of a controlled hammer technique, and secondary flaking along the margins is not very common.

All these open-air sites appear to have been connected with occupational activities. Most of them are associated with granite outcrops rising 5 to 10m above the plains. The possibility of obtaining a commanding view of the surrounding plains, the availability of hard ground for habitational purposes, and the ubiquity of boulders for raising shelters could all have been considerations which influenced Mesolithic settlers to select these outcrops as locales for their encampments. Also noteworthy is the nearness of the sites to stream. The dense forests and hills around should have provided a variety of game and wild plant foods. The raw materials for stone tool-making may have been obtained from nearby veins and dykes, and riverbeds.

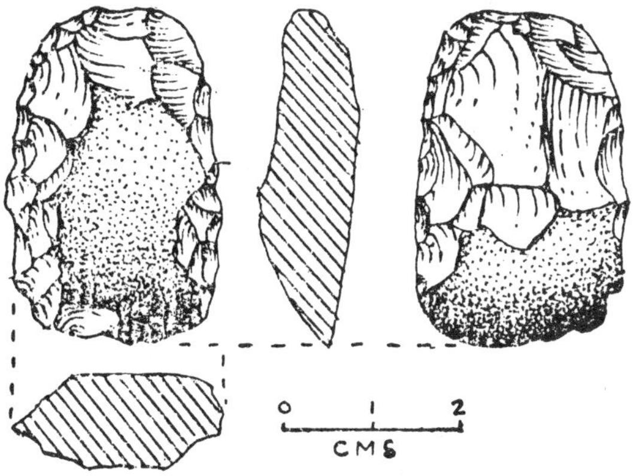

Fig. 1. Miniature adze

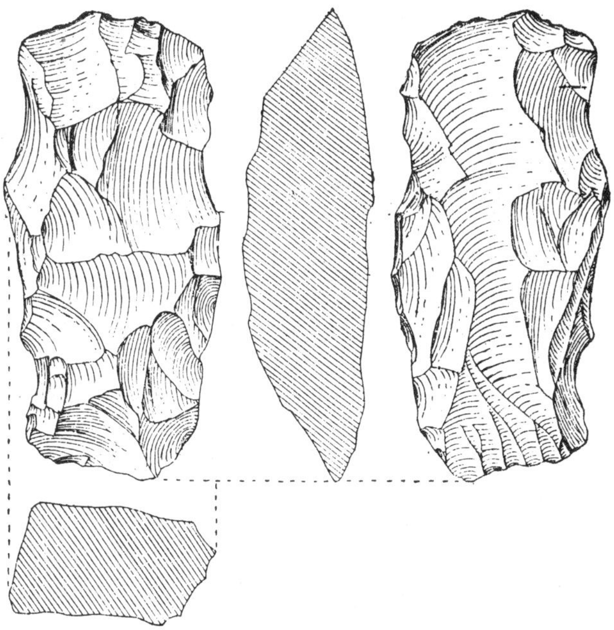

Fig. 3. Double edged axe

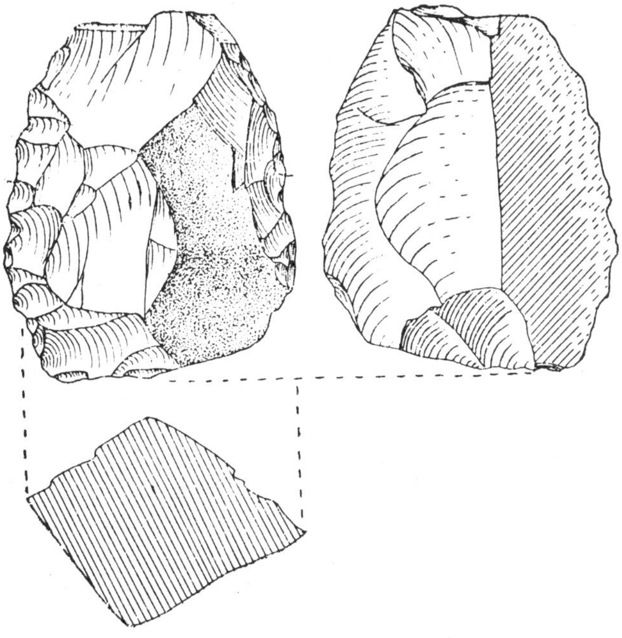

Fig. 2. Core scraper

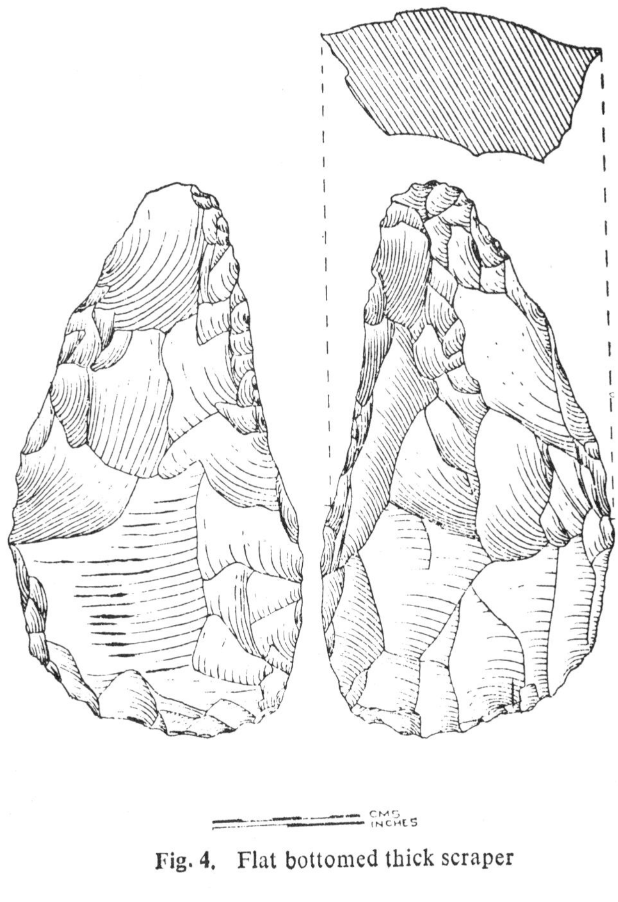

Fig. 4. Flat bottomed thick scraper

13

Excavations at Daulatpur (District Bulandshahar) and its significance

R.C. Gaur

The site of Daulatpur (24°1′ N; 78° 11′ E) was excavated in 1984-85 which turned out to be a camp-site of the OCP period. This site is situated at a distance of about 50 km from Aligarh in District Bulandshahar on the left side of Dibai-Jahangirabad road, and is about 15 km away from the well-known OCP site of Lal Qila on the east. The location of this site has certainly increased our knowledge about the OCP people.

During the course of extensive explorations several OCP sites were located on the bank of Kalinadi a tributary of Ganga at short distances from each other. Some of them being at a distance of 1 to 3 km away from the present course of the river. It appears that once all these sites were along the old course. The river has not changed its course entirely but at places made deviations leaving the old course at some considerable distance. Though Kalinadi is not a turbulent river and normally has a slow water flow, during floods it spreads far wide covering a large area. It appears that this was its main characteristic even in the past. Obviously during the annual floods the OCP using-people would have then been forced to leave their habitations and shift elsewhere temporarily until the water receded. We were therefore, in search of such OCP sites which were temporary seasonal settlements lying beyond the possible flood zone.

The site of Daulatpur was located on the bank of an ancient lake where OCP people shifted their settlements during the rainy and flood seasons. The site has yielded remains of floors, mud-structures, post-holes of hutments and fire places along with broken pottery, terracotta, stone objects, etc.

The site looks is a low mound covering an area of about 240 x 190 metres. On the north-west the lake had a slope and the rainwater could extend to a great distance. Therefore, the people who shifted here from different places preferred to stay mainly on the eastern side of the lake and each group selected its own place for the encampment for habitation. Due to successive settlements the deposit varied at places from 0.75m to 1.50 m in thickness; several floors have been traced out with a large number of post-holes. These post-holes indicate that such hutments, made of wattle and daub, were of different types and sizes viz. circular, rectangular and square. The partition walls of these hutments were some times plastered. Evidence of mud-walls has also been found. It appears that low mud-walls were raised around the huts to prevent rain water entering in. At some places fire-pits were also noticed. The floors of these hutments have mostly been damaged and in some cases only a portion is extant. A few pieces of burnt-bricks were also found indicating that they were also used sporadically.

Since the site was abandoned deliberately after every rainy season, we could not find either good pottery or antiquities. Only those pieces which got damaged during the course of use or shifting and thrown away at the site were found.

However, we found about 8000 such sherds representing piece of storage jars, vases, vessels, bowls, basins, lids, etc. Many of them bear nice slip and are decorated with incised designs and paintings in black pigment. A majority of them are wheel-made having medium fabric. They are generally well-fired. On the whole the pottery of Daulatpur resembles those found at Lal Qila, a site not very far away from this place. It may be recalled that Kiratpur another site in the vicinity had yielded a Copper Hoard implement.

The antiquities found include broken pieces of balls, weights, querns and pestles of stone and balls, beads, wheels of terracotta and pottery discs. Several indeterminate objects were also found.

It appears that this site was a camp site for considerable period are tentatively may be dated to a long time bracket of 2500 and 1500 B.C. On the basis or comparative excavated remains with those found at Lal Qila. Atranjikhera and other similar sites in the region.

14

Sambara or Trailokyavijaya—Fresh identification

J. Nath

Khara Khoto, the Black Town in Etsin-gol delta in the southernmost region of Inner Mangolia, a famous centre of Buddhist Tantric art, was explored by Sir Aurel Stein during his third expedition to Central Asia in 1914. It is quite evident from the finds of Khara Khoto that people were adherents of esoteric Buddhism. Various tantric gods and goddesses were represented in drawings, paintings, wood carvings etc. bearing influences of Indo-Tibetan and Chinese art styles.

The Stein Collection in the National Museum has a number of art objects from Khara Khoto. Of particular interest is a figure carved on wood in relief (Acc. No. K.K.II. 0312), in the form of small pointed flame with scalloped edge suggestive of flickering. A male deity is shown in *alidha* posture trampling over two sprawling figures; one of them, under the right foot, is holding a skull cup in the hand while the other under the left foot, is holding a battle axe. The main deity holds in his right hand a *vajra* and in the left a bell perhaps marked with *vajra* against the chest. He wears a triangular lower garment and is adorned with a fillet made of skulls, bracelets, and passing over forearm. A triple-headed *khatvanga*, held in the crook of left arm, rises above the shoulder.

The deity is marked with elongated ears, *jatamukuta* showing a high top-knot of hair with a *vajra* in front, and a third eye on the forehead.

Stein has described it as a male deity of Saivite appearance.[1] Andrews has called it a 'male deity' (Siva).[2] Nath has identified it as Trailokyavijaya.[3] The present author is inclined to identify this as Sambara for reason to be cited below. However, Nath's identification of the trampled deities as Mahesvara and Gauri is not tenable, for two deities under the foot are holding skull cup and battle axe which are not the attributes of Mahesvara and Gauri, but of Bhairava and Kalaratri, the deities whom Sambara tramples.

On the other hand the description of Sambara in *Sadhanamala* fits well. The *dhyana* in *Sadhanamala* describes Sambara in the following verses;[4]

Lalatasthakapalani candrardham murdhni dharayet ।
Sanmudra-mundamali ca visvavajri trilocanah ॥
Alidhapadavinyaso visvaksaravivartinim ।
Sabhairavam Kalaratrimarudho vyaghracarmabhrt ॥
Aksobhyasekharah kubjo vajraghantajatanvitah ।
Viro'sau Vajravarahi vajrasrkpurnakapalabhrt ॥
Khatvangamekhala rakta trinetra mundamalini ।
Pancamudra muktakesi digvastra Buddhasekhara ॥

—Dvibhuja-Sambaropadesh Samaptah

"The worshipper should think himself as Sambara with a string of skull over his forehead and the crescent moon on the top. He wears the six auspicious ornaments and a necklace of heads. He shows the *Visvavajra* (on his head-dress) and is three eyed. He stands in the *alidha* attitude and originates from a combination of all the letters of the alphabet. He tramples upon Bhairava and Kalaratri and is clad in tiger skin. He shows the effigy of Aksobhya on his crown and is blue in colour. He carries the *Vajra* and *Ghanta;* has matted hair, displays heroism and is embraced by his Shakti Vajravarahi holding the *vajra* and the *kapala* full of blood. Her girdle is the *khatvanga*, her colour is red and she is three-eyed. She wears a garland of severed heads, is endowed with five auspicious symbols, has dishevelled hair and no garment. She shows the image of Buddha (Vairocana) on her crown".[5]

A great similarity can be seen between the above description in *Sadhanamala* and the relief. The deity is two armed and wears a fillet and a necklace of skulls. Visvavajra can be seen on his head-dress and he is three eyed. He also stands in *alidha* posture and tramples over two figures. One under right foot, with skull cup in hand, can be identified as Bhairava and the other under the right foot, with axe can be identified with Kalaratri. The triangular lower garment can be compared with the tiger skin garment. He carries the *vajra* and the *Ghanta* in his hands, has matted hair and displays heroism.

However there are minor variations. For example

the effigy of Aksobhya on his crown is missing. But there are examples of Sambara without effigy of Aksobhya on the crown. One such sculpture is from Patharghata,[6] Bhagalpur and the other from Orissa, presently housed in the National Museum.[7]

The main argument against this figure being Sambara would be the absence of vajravarahi embracing him. However examples of Sambara without his Shakti are not wanting, e.g., Patharghata and National Museum figures. In India as well as in China and Central Asia the *Yugandha* or Yab-yum forms are rarely represented. This form is more popular in Tibet and Nepal. As this image is from Central Asia Shakti is not shown.

Though the *Khatavanga* is not prescribed as an attribute for Sambara in this *dhyana* but *Nishpannayogavali*[8] mentions *khatavanga* as an attribute for twelve armed Sambara and iconographical representations confirm it.

Thus on the basis of the above arguments this deity can be identified as one of the forms of Sambara.

References

1. Stein, A. *Innermost Asia,* Vol. I, New Delhi 1981, p. 479, Pl. LIII.

2. Andrews, F.M. *Descriptive Catalogue of Antiquities,* Delhi 1981, p. 246.

3. Nath, A. *Buddhist Images and Narratives,* New Delhi 1986, pp. 67-68.

4. Bhattacharya, B. (ed.) *Sadhanamala,* Gaikwad Oriental Series No. 41, Baroda 1968, p. 504.

5. Bhattacharya, B. *The Indian Buddhist Iconography,* Calcutta 1958, p. 161.

6. Huntington S., *The Pala-Sena Schools of Sculpture,* Leiden 1984, fig. 195.

7. Asthana, S.P. A controversial Buddhist Tantric deity : Trailokyavijaya *vis-a-vis* Sambara in Sahai, B. (ed.) *History and Calture* Dr. B.P. Sinha Felicitation Volume, Delhi 1987, p. 167-172.

8. Bhattacharya, B. (ed.) *Nishpannayogavali* of Abhayakargupta, Gaikwad Oriental Series No, 109, Baroda 1949, p. 26

15

Siddhaikavira image from Nalanda

J. Nath

Excavations at Nalanda, a famous centre of Tantrik Buddhism has yielded several stone and metal sculptures which are well known for their elegance and craftsmanship. One such stone sculpture which was found in a small shrine to the north of main shrine at Chaitya site 12, was acquired by the National Museum in the year 1949. The sculpture has been repeatedly published by several art historians who are not unanimous in their identification of this image.

The image represents a Bodhisattva in relief against a stele. He is standing in *dvibhanga* pose on an inverted lotus with his right hand in *varamudra* and left holding a stalk of a full blown lotus, which emerges from the floral scrolls and creepers depicted on the left side at the bottom. The hairdo are stylized and arranged in *jatamukuta* with a high and wide top-knot and the hairlocks are falling on the shoulders. On the crest of the *jata* is shown a Dhyani Buddha seated in *bhumisparsamudra* within a beaded border. He is adorned with various jewelled ornaments, multi-stringed necklace, bracelets, armlets, marked with *makarmukha.* He wears a long sacred thread of beaded strings reaching almost upto the knee. He is dressed in a transparent lower garment secured at the waist with jewelled girdle. The fold of drapery is marked by soft and parallel lines more distinct between the legs. A scarf is tied round the waist with tassels falling on the right side.

His face is marked with a broad forehead, half-closed eyes with eyebrows, elongated earlobes and thick lips. The nose and the lower lip are damaged. The facial expression shows compassion. There is a roundal probably a *chakra* on the palm of right hand. The stele is plain and its border is decorated with floral and geometrical designs. Though the upper portion of stele is broken the top seems to have been semi-circular. The sculpture is almost of life size.

So far the sculpture has been identified as Avalokitesvara Padmapani on the basis of his attribute lotus held in the left hand and the Dhyani Buddha seated on crest has been identified as Amitabha,[1] the spiritual father of Avalokitesvara. Huntington[2] has called it an emanation of Akshobhya, representing his *karuna* aspect, as indicated by lotus flower which the deity holds aloft. However, a close look at this sculpture warrants a different identification, viz., Siddhaikavira, one of the forms of Manjusri, the god of wisdom. The following points emphasise this identification:

1. The Bodhisattva must belong to the family of Dhyani Buddhas shown on the crest. The seated figure of Dhyani Buddha here on the creat is in *bhumisparsa mudra*. Therefore, he cannot be identified as Amitabha, who has never been shown in this *mudra*. On the other hand this *mudra* is associated with Dhyani Buddha Akshobhya to whom Manjusri is associated.

2. The recent researches on Tantra has shown that iconography of the *Jinas* and their Bodhisattvas was well formulated by at least the 4th century; therefore, the argument that this is a representation of Avalokitesvara with the depiction of Jina still in flux, seems unlikely.[3]

3. This identification could be corroborated with the literary text also. On the basis of *sadhanas* in *Sadhanamala* the Bodhisattva can be identified as Siddhaikavira. One of the *Dhyanas* in *Sadhanamala* describes his form thus:[4]

> Siddhaikaviro Bhagwan chandramandalasthah chandropasrayah
> jagadudyotakari dvibhuja ekamukhah suklah vajraparyanki
> divyalankarabhusitah panchavirakasekharah...
> vame nilotpaladharah daksine varadah...
> tato Bhagavato maulau Akshobhyam devatyah pujam kurvanti.

"God Siddhaikavira sits on the orb of the moon, is supported by the moon, and illumines the world. He is two-armed, one-faced and of white colour. He sits in the Vajraparyankasana attitude, and is decked in celestial ornaments. His head is decorated with effigies of the five Dhyani Buddhas.... He carries the *utpala* in the left hand and exhibits the *varada mudra* in the right. The goddesses pay homage to Akshobhya who is on the crown of the God'.[5]

The description in *Sabhanamala* fits well with the image under study. Although only one Dhyani Buddha is shown in the *jata* in this case it is worthwhile to note that there are several examples of Siddhaikavira with Akshobhya only.[6]

A bust of an image from the caves of Panhale Kaji, badly defaced, shows Akshobhya in *bhumisparsa mudra* on the crest of the deity. Although the hands of the deity are broken the full blown lotus is seen on the halo, the stalk of which was probably held in the left hand. This image has been identified as Siddhaikavira.[7]

The Sarnath and Nalanda Siddhaikaviras[8] are similar to this image under investigation in all its attributes. However, these and the one under study do differ in posture from the stipulations enjoined in the *Sadhanamala* where the image has to be shown as seated.

As far as the dating of the deity is concerned there are differences of opinion. Huntington has assigned it to sixth century A.D. i.e , late Gupta period. Few others have dated it to 8th century A.D. But Saraswati has rightly dated it to 7th century A.D. On the basis of the stylistic features one finds that it carries many Gupta elements. The transparent drapery, the *makarmukha* armlet, hairlocks setting on shoulder, the serene face and thick lips recall the Gupta features, but the elongated body, broad face, half-closed eyes, the *jatamukuta* and the necklace would warrant a later date perhaps even after sixth century. But this sculpture is certainly prior to the Palas and may perhaps be assigned to the transition phase between the Guptas and the Palas and can safely be dated to 7th century A.D.

References

1. Saraswati, S.K. *Tantrayana Art Album*, Calcutta, 1977 p. xxviii, fig. 48.
2. Huntington, S. *The Pala-Sena Schools of Sculpture*, Leiden, 1984, pp. 17-18.
3. *Ibid.*, p. 18.
4. Bhattacharya, B. *Sadhanamala*, Gaikward Oriental Series No. 26, Baroda 1968, p. 140.
5. Bhattacharya, B. *The Indian Buddhist Iconography*, Calcutta 1958, p. 113-114.
6. Saraswati, *op cit.* fig. 12 and 24.
7. Deshpande, M.N. *The Caves of Panhale-Kaji*, New Delhi 1986, p. 137, pl. 68.
8. Saraswati, *op. cit.* fig. 12 and 24.

16

A New Light on Jhusi Culture in Allahabad, U.P.

R.S. Rana

The site Jhusi (Lat. 25°29'N, Long. 81°55E') or Pratishthanapura of the Puranas is situated on the left bank of the Ganga, opposite the confluence of the Ganga and the Yamuna.

Several localities such as Purani Jhusi, Maheen, Akela Peda, Muhammadabad, Chhatanag. Munshi ki Bagia, Nimi Kalan and Bajaha, go to make Jhusi. Many gullies criss-cross every mound and run from north to south. The gullies reveal the sections; the index of cultural *milieu*.

I have visited the site and seen different layers in the deposit in the left bank of the river Ganga and they, from top to bottom are kanker bed, reddish yellow silt, gravel formation, plastic clay and last is the yellowish sandy deposit respectively, embodying archaeological antiquities from pre-N.B.P. to post-N.B.P. periods.

Different animal bones indicate the several species of animals that were domesticated in the historical period. *Bos indicus*, cattle femur, distal end, sheep, goat and pigs, etc. are some of the animal bones.

Beautiful sculptural pieces are seen in the houses of every villages. Lotus, a lion half-broken, dancing scene are fitted in the wall of Dargah Sharif of Purani Jhusi nearby the protectedsite of Samudrakupa.

Terracottas of the Gupta period are fitted in a wall of the Nageshwar temple in Chhatanag. Terracottas viz. Kubera-head, Bangles, important potsherds, iron objects, fossils, red ware mini *lota* have been picked up from Nimi Kalan.

There are several mounds which are demarcated by gullies in the village Nimi Kalan. Surface of the mound indicates the importance of the site which is situated in the north-eastern side about one km from river Ganga. Two neoliths are worshipped with Lord Siva in the village Nimi Kalan.

A couple on ivory plaque of Kushana period, a gold coin of Kumaragupta, a silver coin of Skandagupta are preserved in the Museum of Allahabad. An inscription discovered from Chhatanag describes the donation of curd, milk in the holy bank in Nagtirtha provides holy merit for the donor. The inscription, in Sanskrit relates to 86 pair of Nagas.

Indian scriptures *Mahabharata*, *Bhagavata Purana* and *Matsya Purana* speak about Jhusi as Pratishtanapura and its legendary king is Pururava. The story of Urvasi and Pururava is famous in ancient Indian literature.

Book Review

P. Banerjee : *Rama in Indian Literature Art and Thought*, Sundeep Prakashan, Delhi 1986. Two volumes, containing respectively text and illustrations. Price Rs. 1,100

India is a highly religion-oriented country, and whatever one might think about the city-dwellers in this regard, the vast rural population that constitutes real India bears an ample testimony to the foregoing statement. One has only to visit Allahabad or Hardwar on the occasion of the *Kumbha Melas*, or Mathura on *Janmashtami* or Ayodhya on *Rama-Navami* to get a feel of how religion has gone into the very bones of the Hindus. (And the same is true in respect of the followers of Islam and other religions.)

The present writer had occosions to be in Ayodhya on *Rama-Navami* days and found it almost impossible even to inch his way, because of the immense human wave that floods Ayodhya from far and near on that day. Indeed, if one were to take an aerial photograph of the township around mid-day, the time of Shri Rama's birth, one would not be able to get on the photograph any of the streets of Ayodhya. Instead, one would find millions of human heads carrying a little bundle of some sort of clothings and food-stuff. They arrive there the previous evening footing long distances, have a bath in the Sarayu in the morning of *Rama-Navami* and march towards Kanak Bhawan where the main function relating to Shri Rama's birth is celebrated.

Such is the spell that Shri Rama has cast on the Hindus, be they in the north or south or east or west. Indeed, the Rama-cult has found its way even to distant lands—Thailand, Indonesia, etc. on the one hand and Central Asia on the other.

Thus, a book dealing with the story of Shri Rama in all its aspects and bringing out pictorially the manner in which this story has influenced not only literature but also various categories of fine arts, such as sculptures, paintings, bronzes, etc. is a most welcome addition to any library. (The price, Rs. 1,100, is almost prohibitive for any individual, except perhaps a few blessed by the goddess Lakshmi.) Dr. P. Banerjee, the author, had done an equally commendable job some ten years ago by bringing out an almost similar book on the life of Shri Krishna.

Volume I of the book under consideration here is divided into three chapters, dealing respectively with : 1, The *Ramayana*, its Importance, Influence and Popularity; 2, Rama story in Valmiki's *Ramayana* and 3, Ramayana Tradition in Different Regions of India. There are also three appendices : A, Rama-katha in Buddhist Literature; B, Jaina Rama-katha; and C, Persian Ramayana. The three appendices, it may incidentally be observed, show that the Rama story finds a place not only in non-Hindu texts, such as Buddhist and Jain, but also in a language of foreign origin, viz. the Persian.

Volume II contains 284 illustrations depicting paintings on paper, wood and walls, terracottas, stuccos, stone-sculpture and bronzes. These also cover a very wide span both in time and space. While the earliest examples go back to the second century B. C., the latest ones belong to our own century. In space, the coverage is from Jammu and Kashmir in the north to Kerala in the south and from Gujarat in the west to Assam in the east. Also included are some extra-Indian examples—from Central Asia in the north-west and Indonesia in the south-east. All these illustrations have been put in a sequence which unfolds the life-story of Shri Rama. This is quite a sensible way of organizing the various media. Talking of the paintings, one feels the absence of coloured plates, since many of the miniature paintings do have an excellent colour-combination. The publishers should not have grudged the little extra expenditure on a few such plates, since as already stated, he has priced the publication pretty high.

Of special interest is the portrayal of Rama and Sita on the silver coins of Akbar, assignable to the closing years of the king's reign (Pls. 278-79). Incidentaly, this is one more evidence of the catholic outlook of the emperor.

In passing one may draw attention to Plate 277.

According to the caption, it depicts Rama, Lakshmana and Sita whereas there is only one (central) male figure. Perhaps something has gone wrong somewhere.

Nearly half of the text-pages (Chapter II, pp. 37-171 out of a total of 277) are devoted to the Rama story as given in Valmiki's *Ramayana*. This being by and large a re-narration of the story does not call for any kind of review. It is only the other two chapters that can invite some sort of discussion. However, since in a short review like the present one full-length discussions are not possible, one may perhaps touch upon just a couple of issues.

As is well known, there is a debate, a rather heated one, about the historicity of the two personages, Krishna and Rama. While according to some, both the epics, the *Mahabharata* and the *Ramayana*, are the figments of poetic imagination, others believe that everything in these texts is correct to the very letter, so much so that they hold that Shri Rama, after his conquest of Lanka, did travel back to Ayodhya in an aeroplane. In addition, there is another kind of debate, viz. who preceded the other, Krishna or Rama? In respect of these debates, Banerjee seems to hold that both Krishna and Rama were historical figures and that while Krishna lived in the fifteenth century B.C., Rama may have lived in the nineteenth or twentieth century B.C. (pp. 9-11).

The readers would perhaps like to know the archaeological evidence in this regard. Intensive excavations and extensive explorations of the sites associated with the Mahabharata and Ramayana stories have established two very significant points viz.

(i) that, but for an isolated exception here or there, *none of these sites is earlier than circa eleventh century B.C.* and (ii) that *all the Mahabharata sites are consistently earlier than the Ramayana ones.*

The present writer would leave it to the readers to draw their own conclusions from the aforesaid archaeological evidence. (Those further interested in the topic are invited to have a look at : B.B. Lal, The Two Indian Epics vis-a-vis Archaeology, *Antiquity*, Vol. LV, 1981, pp. 27-34.)

Amongst the various pieces of evidence often quoted to support the precedence of Rama over Krishna, is the one relating to the occurrence of *Ramopakhyana* in the *Mahabharata*. The present writer would like to bring to the notice of scholars a piece of evidence which points in the opposite direction : it is a reference to Krishna in the *Ramayana*.

In the *Yuddha-kanda*, which is never regarded as a later addition like the *Bala-kanda* and *Uttara-kanda*, it is mentioned that just when Sita was about to enter the fire in order to establish her chastity, various gods such as Varuna, Siva, Brahma appeared on the scene and reminded Rama of his previous incarnations in which Sita, under other names, had been his faithful consort. Hence, they advised him, he should not doubt her chastity. *Among these earlier incarnations is that of Krishna* as well. The relevant verses are as follows :

Lokanam tvam paro dharmo Vishvakasenaschaturbhujah ।
Sarngadhanva Hrishikeshah purushah purushottamah ॥ (VI, 120, 15)
Ajitah khadgadhrig Vishnuh KRISHNA schaiva Brihadbalah ।
Sita Lakshmirbhavan Vishnurdevah KRISHNAH Prajapatih ॥ (VI, 120, 16)
Vadhartham Ravanasyeha pravishto manushim tanum । (VI, 120, 28)
Tadidam na kritam karyam tvaya dharmabhritamvara
Nihato Ravano Rama prahrishto divamakrama ॥ (VI, 120, 29)

Drawing attention to certain well known West Asian epigraphs of the fifteenth and fourteenth centuries B.C., which mention the names of Vedic gods like Indra, Varuna, etc. and of princes like Sutarna, Dusratta, Artatama, etc., Banerjee concludes :

"The above facts reveal beyond doubt the presence of Aryans in West Asia. What is of special interest to us is the name of 'Dusratta' mentioned above. The Sanskrit form of Dusratta is definitely Dasaratha, who may perhaps be the same as the father of Rama." (p. 12)

Now, even if the equation of the word 'Dusratta' with Dasaratha be all right, why must he be necessarily the father of Rama ? There is not even the slightest indication to that effect in any of these epigraphs, nor in any contemporary or near-contemporary text of West Asia. If such *base*-less suggestions are made and accepted, why should one laugh at the suggestion once made by a scholar that king Ramases of Egypt was none other than Rama of the Ramayana story ? Indeed, there should be a limit to sound-philology, which may not always be sound.

The present writer is sorry to have picked holes in an otherwise very useful publication. Indeed, the scholarly world will always remain grateful to Dr. P. Banerjee for these volumes on *Rama in Indian Literature, Art and Thought*, as it has been for the Krishna volumes.

B.B. LAL

WORLD ARCHAEOLOGICAL CONGRESS
STEERING COMMITTEE MEETING
HELD AT CUMANA, VENEZUELA

Meeting of the World Archaeological Congress Steering Committee Held at the Cumanagoto Hotel, Cumana, Venezuela on 19 & 20 October 1987

MINUTES

Present: Professor M H Day (Chair)
Mrs C K Cane
Mr R Cruz (Observer)
Professor J—M Essomba
Professor E Eyo (alternate for Professor B W Andah)
Professor J Golson
Ms J Hammil
Dr K Kristiansen (Observer)
Professor M Sanoja
Mr P G Stone
Professor P J Ucko (Secretary)
Professor M Zamora (alternate for Professor An Zhimin)

Mr P A Crake
Ms J Hudert

Apologies:

Professor D P Agrawal
Professor An Zhimin
Professor D Dincauze
Dr V P Shilov

Absent:

Professor B W Andah

The Chair and the Secretary reported to the Steering Committee the reasons for the absence of the missing Steering Committee members and the statuses of those who had been invited to attend.

Professor Agrawal had had to return to India because of his wife's illness, and had nominated Dr S P Gupta as his alternate, but he in turn was not able to participate due to British visa problems. Therefore a representative for South Asia was not present, although the Chair had received a telegram of support for any decision taken by the Steering Committee.

Professor An Zhimin was not able to participate and had agreed that the Chair should nominate an alternative representative for East Asia. Professor M Zamora had kindly agreed to act as his alternate.

Dr VP Shilov had apparently not been informed of the meeting and was unable to attend at short notice, and had therefore also agreed that the Chair should nominate an alternative representative for eastern Europe, but time had not allowed this to happen.

Professor D Dincauze was too busy to participate but had said that she was available to be contacted by telephone at work or at home, and she had consulted at least with Dr Kristiansen. An alternate for north America had therefore not been sought.

Professor B W Andah had not responded to several telegrams in sufficient time to ensure his participation, and so Professor E Eyo had been nominated by the Chair as his alternate (the former being the Secretary and the latter the President of the Pan-African Congress on Prehistory and Related Subjects).

Dr K Kristiansen was present as an observer, also representing the International Committee on Archaeological Heritage Management. Mr R Cruz was also present as an observer, assisting Ms J Hammil. A representative of the World Council of Indigenous Peoples had also been invited to be present as an observer, but had not been able to attend. Mr P Crake was present as Minutes Secretary, and Ms J Hubert was present as his assistant.

The Steering Committee agreed to the observer statuses as outlined by the Chair. Observers would be able to participate freely in the meeting, but would not have a vote.

1. Confirmation of the minutes of the meeting of 21-23 January 1987

The previously circulated Minutes were accepted as a true record, and signed by the Chair.

2. Matters arising

A Matters Arising document (attached) was tabled by the Secretary for information, and accepted.

3. Report of the Mainz Congress

Taken together with :

4. Current Situation—IUPPS's Apparent Rejection of Steering Committee's Requests

The Secretary reported that both the Secretary-General and the President of IUPPS had been presented with a list of minimum and maximum requests for changes to the Statutes, together with a demand that South Africans be removed from the Permanent Council of the organisation; most members of the Permanent Council of the IUPPS had also been similarly circulated. The WAC had also suggested that the IUPPS should discuss the problems of archaeology and the treatment of human remains. All these written communications had been addressed impersonally to the Secretary-General and to the President, given that there was still doubt over the incumbency of these positions.

The Representative of Papua New Guinea on the Permanent Council, Professor Les Groube, had put formal written motions to the IUPPS, supported by more than the necessary ten signatures of other members of the IUPPS Permanent Council, demanding that the suggested changes to the Statutes be formally considered by the Permanent Council. The Minutes of the May meeting of the International Executive of the IUPPS in Czechoslovakia had rejected all but one of the minor suggested revisions. A detailed summary of the main responses by the International Executive Committee was tabled, and the Secretary highlighted their character and quality, in particular their insistence on IUPPS tradition, their refusal to countenance a role for anyone who was not a *professional* archaeologist, and the Secretary-General's rejection of preferential financial support for Third World members of the IUPPS. These responses from the IUPPS Executive Committee were discussed at considerable length.

Sir David Wilson had reported that at the Mainz Congress the Permanent Council had decided to set up a Statutes Working Group to recommend to the Permanent Council any changes that might be considered necessary. A motion put by him that the Statutes Working Group should consult with the World Archaeological Congress Steering Committee had been rejected, but the Statutes Working Group had been instructed to consult as widely as it wished. However, the majority of the membership of the Group was antagonistic to the WAC and its suggestions, and to any proposals for fundamental change.

It was understood that the first meeting of the Permanent Council in Mainz had only some 30 members present and the second only some 21.

Dr Kristiansen confirmed this whole account from his own discussions with members of the Permanent Council.

The Chair reported that the only concrete result of his various letters to the IUPPS Secretary-General was that Professor Nenquin had written to him indicating that he would only be prepared to talk with WAC from a position that "*all* scholars must participate, irrespective of nationality".

The Secretary also reminded the Steering Committee that the only response of UNESCO to his long and detailed outline of the situation between the WAC and the IUPPS had been that it was an internal matter for IUPPS to sort out.

The Chair tabled copies of a letter he had received from Mr Mturi, one of the Tanzanian Representatives on the Permanent Council, who had been present at both of the Permanent Council meetings in Mainz. This letter appeared to indicate that the IUPPS Executive Committee had *privately* agreed to remove the South Africans from the Permanent Council, but the Chair and others believed that this could not, in fact, have been the case. In fact the IUPPS General Assembly at Mainz had passed the following motion :

> that the IUPPS reaffirms its total commitment to academic freedom. The IUPPS refuses any form of discrimination based on the concept of race, philosophical conviction, nationality, sex, language, etc, discrimination which by its intolerance and by definition, is the negation itself of any form of co-operation. The IUPPS confirms that it cannot exclude any *bona fide* scholar from its meetings, and that individual participation of any scholar in a congress/colloquia/symposia can in no way be considered as an acceptance by the IUPPS of the political regime in which the scholars work.

Although this motion could be interpreted as referring only to individual South African participants in Congresses, and not necessarily also to representatives of South Africa on the Permanent Council, Professor Golson believed that there was no doubt that the substantive response that had come out of the IUPPS was its refusal to co-operate with the WAC Steering Committee or to contemplate any real change to its structure or proceedings.

The Chair emphasized that there had been no official representatives of the Steering Committee at Mainz, but that Professor Ucko, Mrs Cane and Mr Stone had attended in their personal capacities. Mr Stone tabled copies of an article written by him from the University of Southampton's magazine, entitled "Memories are Made of This : Reflections on Mainz", and gave a detailed verbal account of what had happened at the Mainz meetings. Mr Stone described the apparent administrative chaos of the Congress, and the statements made at the series of public debates and meetings organized by a local consortium of students, and political and trade union groups. It was noted that Anti-Apartheid demonstrations had received as much press and radio coverage as the activities of the congress itself and that the IUPPS Permanent Council representative of Mozambique had declared publicly that he could not attend either the IUPPS Permanent Council meeting nor the congress because of the presence of South Africans. Mr Stone estimated that only some 400 people had been present at the Mainz congress. However, the Mainz organizers had refused to give out lists of the names of those people who were actually present, and their published list of participants was self-evidently inaccurate. The Secretary reported that one of the Indian members of the Permanent Council had reported to him that the IUPPS Statutes Working Group was just a smoke-screen for non-activity, and that Third World members of the IUPPS should now withdraw. The Secretary also reported that several participants at the Mainz congress had approached him to urge the Steering Committee to go ahead with a new, and more relevant, world archaeological organization.

It was understood that Spain had withdrawn its offer to host the next IUPPS Congress, and that Israel and Czechoslovakia had offered to host the 1991 meeting. The Slovak Academy of Science had guaranteed the participation at the Congress of *all bona fide* scholars. However, the ANC understood that the Czechoslovakian Government would not in fact issue any visas to South Africans to attend the 1991 IUPPS Congress.

It was understood that new representatives of China, Australia, and several other countries had now joined the Permanent Council.

The Chair summarised the position which had been reached :

the Executive Committee of the IUPPS had rejected the suggested revisions to the Statutes;

the Permanent Council had not rejected those suggestions, but had instead set up a Working Group to consider the IUPP's Statutes, and to report back in two years' time to the next Permanent Council.

After much discussion of this position, the question whether or not the brief of the WAC Plenary Session had been fully carried out, and the implications of different possible courses of action, Professor Zamora proposed the following motion, which was seconded by Professor Sanoja :

that in view of the serious efforts made by the Steering Committee to negotiate with the IUPPS, and in view of the failure of negotiations as reported by the Chair and Secretary of the Steering Committee : a World Archaeological Congress organization be established to fulfil the mandate established by more than 500 of the World Archaeological Congress's participants in their Plenary Session in Southampton.

This motion was carried unanimously, and with the full support of the observers.

Mrs Cane drew the Committee's attention to the words of the Plenary Session's Chairman (page 23) : "...if there is no agreement from the IUPPS, the temporary Steering Committee has a mandate to start a new organization".

5. Actions to be Taken

5. (a) United Nations
(c) ANC/SWAPO
(d) IUPPS Permanent Council
(g) Constituencies of WAC

The Secretary tabled a document suggesting some possible foundations for the establishment of a new World Archaeological Congress organization. After lengthy discussion about the possible relationships between the IUPPS and WAC, it was agreed that the WAC would be set up as an independent organization which would not seek to confront or to replace the IUPPS, but which would promote the new world archaeology and the "humane face of archaeology", interests which were not represented in any other organization. The consensus was for a neutral attitude to the IUPPS and its Permanent Council : this would not preclude the World Archaeological Congress from having, for example, joint meetings with Commissions of the IUPPS.

The Committee reaffirmed its commitment to taking action in the exceptional case of the apartheid regime of South Africa by following the resolutions of the UN/UNESCO, but noted with interest that the ANC/SWAPO might modify their stand about a total cultural and academic boycott of South Africa on a future occasion.

The Chair summarized the requirements for a new organization :

that the new WAC organization would be primarily based on individual Membership, and its success therefore depended on individual enthusiasms;

that Members of the WAC should be involved in the workings of the organization;

that the new WAC organization would not be limited to pre-and proto-history;

that the concerns of the new WAC organization would include "social archaeology";

that the executive body of the new organization should be small enough to be effective, but large enough to ensure true representation;

that the executive body should primarily be based on regional representation;

that the executive body should give due weight to Third and Fouth World opinions;

that those on the executive body should have clear constituencies, and that they should have limited tenure (but be eligible for re-election);

that those on the executive body should represent the young as well as the established, and that there should be a balance of the sexes; and

that archaeology has a social as well as an academic role, and that, as such, it should take a stance on human rights issues as defined by the UN/UNESCO.

After further discussion it was agreed to adjourn the meeting to allow the Secretary to produce a draft preamble for a World Archaeological Congress organization in the light of the comments made during the discussions, to be tabled when the Steering Committee reassembled the following morning.

The Steering Committee adjourned to 09 : 00 on 20 October

The Secretary tabled a draft Preamble for a new World Archaeological Congress organization. After much discussion it was agreed to request the Secretary to amend the document bearing in mind the comments made by the Steering Committee. It was agreed that that document would then form the basis for the new organization.

The Chair then suggested that the Agenda be re-arranged to take into account those areas which had already been covered by the meeting.

The following Agenda order was then agreed :

5. (b) UNESCO
   (x) Other meetings and organizations
   (e) Czechoslovakia
   (f) IUAES
   (h) Human remains
   (i) Return of cultural property
   (j) World Archaeological Bulletin 2 and South Africa
6. The Second Congress of the World Archaeological Congress, and Inter-congresses, and the World Archaeological Congress organization
7. Finance
8. Any Other Business.

5. Actions to be taken

5. (b) UNESCO

It was agreed that it would be courteous to inform UNESCO at this time that the Streering Committee had agreed to set up a new organization to cater for the kind of archaeology with which it was concerned. Any formal relationship with UNESO which might be sought at a future date would be a matter for the new World Archaeological Congress executive body. It was noted that "official" recognition of the new WAC would probably facilitate the granting of funds to those who wished to attend its congresses.

5. (e) Czechoslovakia

It was agreed that the Steering Committee as such should not express any opinion about the proposed IUPPS Congress in Czechoslovakia in 1991.

5. (x) Other Meetings and Organizations

It was agreed to take no formal action over the proposed IUPPS International Executive Committee meeting in Leningrad in 1990.

Professor Eyo stated that if the Egyptians followed Professor Desmond Clark's lead and permitted South African participation at the next Pan-African Congress meeting, scheduled for Cairo in 1988, then a new Pan-African organization would have to be set up. Both he and Professor Essomba were very critical of Professor Clark's belated claims that the Jos meeting's decisions had been unconstitutional. It was agreed that the Chair should write a letter to the Pan-African Congress supporting its stand against South African participation as democratically decided at the Jos meeting.

The Secretary pointed out to the Steering Committee that a new journal had been established called the *Journal of World Prehistory*, apparently by people who are antagonistic to the general aims of WAC.

5. (f) IUAES

It was agreed that it would be courteous to inform the IUAES that the Streering Committee had agreed to set up a new organization to cater for the kind of archaeology with which it is concerned. It was agreed to defer consideration of any formal relationship with the IUAES to a meeting of the new World Archaeological Congress executive body.

5. (h) and (i) Human remains and the Return of cultural property

It was decided to consider these items under Agenda item 6.

5. (j) World Archaeological Bulletin 2 and South Afica

The Secretary reported that Mr Crake, the Editor of World Archaeological Bulletin, had received a letter from a South African requesting that she be allowed to receive future copies of the Bulletin. It was agreed that South Africans would not be permitted to become members of the World Archaeological Congress organization while the UN/UNESCO called for a total ban on cultural contacts with South African/Namibia, but that as the Bullentin would be offered for sale through normal commercial outlets she would be able to deal with the book-sellers in the normal way.

6. Second Congress of the World Archaeological Congress, and Intercongresses, and the World Archaeological Congress Organization

After much discussion of various possibilities regarding locations and funding in Venezuela, the Steering Committee formally requested Professor Mario Sanoja to organize the second World Archaeological Congress in Venezuela in September 1990.

The Committee agreed that Venezuela was very much the first choice for the location of the next Congress but that it should also seek an alternative in case it did not prove possible to mount the next Congress there. It was agreed that Professor Essomba should contact the Centre International des Civilisations Bantu (CICIBA) in Gabon to discuss whether they would be able to hold the Congress in 1990 should Venezuela not be able to accept the Committee's offer, and/or whether they would wish to organize the third World Archaeological Congress scheduled for 1994.

The Secretary tabled a document relating to the Waigani Seminar scheduled to take place in Port Moresby, Papua New Guinea, in September 1988. After much discussion it was agreed to request the organizers of the Waigani Seminar to allow the association of the name of the World Archaeological Congress with their sub-theme on "culture houses", and that this should form the 1988 World Archaeological Congress Inter-Congress meeting. The occasion of this Inter-Congress would also be the time for the first meeting of the proposed new WAC executive body.

Ms Hammil announced that in September 1989 the University of South Dakota would be happy to host an Inter-Congress of the World Archaeological Congress in association with American Indians Against Desecration and the International Indian Treaty Council, to discuss the treatment by archaeologists of human remains. Such a meeting should involve archaeologists from all over the world, including those not sympathetic to the position of indigenous peoples. The Committee welcomed this offer.

After much further discussion the Committee agreed the details of the main lines of the aims, structure and organization of the new World Archaeological Congress and requested the Secretary to draw up a document from which draft Acts could be prepared for consideration at the 1990 WAC Council meeting. The following document has been agreed in draft by full members of the Steering Committee, has been issued to the press, and will be the basis for action through World Archaeological Bulletin 2.

The World Archaeological Congress

1. AIMS

There is a need for a new world organization that recognises the changes which have occurred in the subject of archaeology over the part years, changes which are not reflected in, nor constitute a significant focus of, the existing international body for prehistoric and protohistoric sciences, the International Union of Prehistoric and Protohistoric Sciences.

The World Archaeological Congress is concerned with all aspects of archaeological theory and practice. Its main emphasis is on the academic issues and questions which benefit from a widely oriented and comparative approach. It attempts to bridge the disciplinary divisions of the past into chronological periods (such as prehistoric or protohistoric or historic archaeology) and to avoid exclusive, particularistic regional concerns.

The World Archaeological Congress is based on the explicit recognition of the historical and social role, and political context of, archaeological enquiry, of archaeological organizations, and of archaeological interpretation. Its distinctive aims are :

(1) to discuss themes which truly reflect the interest of its world-wide membership;
(2) to make explicit the relevance of its studies to the wider community.

Within this framework of interest, the World Archaeological Congress does not consider itself to be exclusive to *bona fide* scientists, but a forum for discussion for all those who are genuinely concerned with the study of the past.

The World Archaeological Congress has already identified several areas (which are neither intended to be exhaustive nor exclusive), on which it hopes to focus attention at its future Congress and Inter-Congresses. These include (in no particular order) :

1. education about the past;
2. the role and control of the past in the creation of gender and group and regional and national identity;
3. the ownership, conservation and exploitation of the archaeological heritage;
4. the treatment and disposition of human remains;
5. the funding, organisation, control and choice of archaeological research projects;
6. the effects of archaeology on host communities;
7. the ethics of archaeological enquiry.

The World Archaeological Congress recognises that Many of its Members will naturally also be concerned with specialist regional and chronological subjects, including historical and culture-specific investigations. It therefore envisages specialist meetings carried out under the aegis of the World Archaeological Congress, sometimes in collaboration with existing organizations such as the International Committee on Archaeological Heritage Management, the International Union for Quaternary Research, specialist Commissions of the International Union of Anthropological and Ethnological Sciences; and particularly through its own Institutional Members. The Congresses and Inter-Congresses of the World Archaeological Congress may also establish specialist working groups with their own memberships in order to carry out in-depth considerations of restricted specialist topics.

The World Archaeological Congress has also defined its role beyond its essential academic functions and appreciates that archaeology has a social, as well as an academic, responsibility and, in the context of apartheid, as exemplified by the regime of the Republic of South Africa, recognises the need for it to support, and to be seen to support, the United Nations' and the United Nations Educational, Scientific and Cultural Organization's resolutions on human rights. This is not the only aspect of an "humane archaeology" which is the basis of the

World Archaeological Congress's activities, for the World Archaeological Congress also recognises the importance of archaeological evidence about the past to the rights and aspirations of those directly affected by archaeology. While recognising the essential role of the past to group identity of many peoples and "ethnic groups" who have moved, for whatever reasons, from land to land, the World Archaeological Congress considers that it is the quality of traditional ownership of the land by indigenous peoples which forges an indissoluable link with archaeology, and representatives of these groups have therefore been assigned an effective role, as of right, on the World Archaeological Congress's Executive and Council.

2. Organization

The World Archaeological Congress's success or failure is dependent, as an organization, not only on Institutional Membership but especially on the commitment of individuals to Individual Membership of this new body.

The World Archaeological Congress does not wish to challenge the particular interests and specialisations of existing institutions and organizations. It is new not only in concept but also in its organization and structure. The World Archaeological Congress will operate within distinctive parameters:

1. its Executixe will be of a size which enables it to act really effectively;
2. its Executive will be composed of a combination of:
   (a) Regional Members (elected democratically for a limited period but eligible for re-election); and
   (b) Representatives of indigenous peoples/the Fourth World (appointed for a limited period but eligible for re-appointment);
3. its Executive will include representatives of the senior and of the junior, with regard to a balance between the sexes.
4. its Council will come into being only for the period of each Congress of the World Archaeological Congress, and will comprise the Executive and, in addition, one National Member per country (selected for the duration of the proceedings of a Congress by the Congress participants of each nation);
5. its Officers will consist of a President, Secretary and Treasurer who shall be elected at one Congress and hold office until the next. Any Individual Member of the World Archaeological Congress shall be eligible for nomination, and voters will be the Members of Council. Those elected who are not already Executive or Council Members will automatically become full Members of the Executive and Council. [Until the first Council meeting in 1990 the current office holders of the World Archaeological Congress will continue in office and will be full Members of the Executive.]

The organization of the Congresses of the World Archaeological Congress are distinct from the World Archaeological Congress's own structure, their relationship being provided by annual reports from the Congress's Organizing Committee to the World Archaeological Congress's Executive.

3. Institutional and Individual Membership

Institutions or individuals with a genuine interest in, or concern for, the past may become members of the World Archaeological Congress by completion of an application form and the payment of an agreed subscription.

Annual subscription for membership of US $20 (Individuals), US $10 (Students), and US $100 (Institutions), has been agreed, subject to periodic review by the Council. The Executive will be responsible for any waiving of, or modifications to, particular subscription dues, as well as for any terminations of memberships.

Individual Membership of the World Archaeological Congress includes:

1. eligibility to form part of a regionally defined Electoral College;

2. eligibility to be nominated as a Regional Representative to the Executive/Council;
3. attendance at Congresses and Inter-Congresses at a concessionary registration fee;
4. eligibility to be nominated as a National Representative to Council;
5. free receipt of the World Archaeological Bulletin;
6. concessionary rates for other activities to be organized by the World Archaeological Congress.

Institutional Membership of the World Archaeological Congress includes:

1. free receipt of the World Archaeological Bulletin, and concessionary rates for any other publications;
2. participation in the organization of appropriate general and specialist meetings of the World Archaeological Congress.

4. Some of the World Archaeological Congress's Activities Planned for the Future

1. Publication of the second World Archaeological Bulletin in December 1987.
2. An Inter-Congress, in association with the Cultural Heritage sub-theme of the Waigani Seminar, on "The Role of 'Cultural Centres/Cultural Houses' in the Presentation and Maintenance of Tradition", Port Moresby, Papua New Guinea, September 1988.
3. An In Inter-Congress, in association with American Indians Against Desecration and the International Indian Treaty Council, on "Archaeological Ethics and the Treat ment of Human Remains", to be held at the University of South Dakota, United States of America, August/September 1989.
4. The second Congress of the World Archaeological Congress, to be held in Venezuela in September 1990 with Professor Mario Sanoja as the Chair of the Organizing Committee, and with Dr Jacqueline Clarac de Briceno as the Director of the Local Committee in Merida.

5. Executive

Five months after the first bulk dispatch of application forms those individuals who have paid their subscriptions will be placed within a Regional Electoral College. At the same time as applying to join as Members, they may nominate *up to two* condidates (who must also be Individual Members of the World Archaeological Congress) for election to the Executive by providing details of the nominee's name, gender, position (and length of time employed in that position and any previous position related to archaeology or the study of the past), together with the name of a seconder and a signed statement of agreement from the nominee.

Those who agree to be nominated to the Executive should be aware that, if elected, they are expected to attend the first meeting of the Executive to be held at the time of the Inter-Congress of the World Archaeogical Congress in Port Meresby, Papua New Guinea, in September 1988. The succesful candidates will be notified of their election by telegram in July 1988.

For the purposes of the World Archaeological Congress elections to its Executive, Individual Members will be initially assigned to Regional Electoral Colleges on the basis of their residence. At the first Council meeting reassignment at the request of Individual Members to different Regional Electoral Colleges on the basis of a proven commitment to ongoing research in a particular area will be considered.

The initial fourteen Regional Electoral Colleges will be :

1. Central Africa
2. Eastern and Southern Africa
3. Northern Africa
4. Western Africa
5. Central America and the Caribbean
6. Northern America

7. Southern America
8. Eastern Asia
9. Southeastern Asia and the Pacific
10. Southern Asia
11. Near and Middle East
12. Eastern Europe and Central Asia
13. Northern Europe
14. Southern Europe.

In June 1988 a secret postal ballot will be conducted through each Regional Electoral College to elect :

1. a Senior Representative (someone who is, or has been, in permanent employment within archaeology, or a related discipline, for more than five years);
2. a Junior Representative.

In effect, therefore, there will be two ballots, one for Senior Representatives and one for Junior Representatives; both will be based on a single transferable voting system. In each ballot *at least three* votes must be cast *in rank order*, of which *at least one* must be for a female candidate *and at least one* must be for a male candidate. This electoral system has been chosen to give substance to the World Archaeological Congress's intention to give balance to senior and to junior, and to both sexe.

Those duly elected will constitute the Executive of the World Archaeological Congress, together with eight Representatives of indigenous peoples/the Fourth World (these Representatives will be chosen by the International Indian Treaty Council, the World Council of Indigenous Peoples, and the United Nations' Working Group on Indigenous Populatations). At its first meeting in 1988 the Executive will elect its own Chair.

At the end of the second Congress of the World Archaeological Congress in 1990 Council will decide which half of the Executive will cease to serve. The remaining half of the Executive will continue until the third Congress of the World Archaeological Congress.

Elections for the vacant half of the Executive will proceed as soon as possible after each Council meeting. Nominations from the Regional Electoral Colleges will only be accepted for nominess from countries in that region not at that time represented on the Executive.

Subsequently, each half of the Executive will serve for a period of eight years.

The Executive will normally meet at least during each of the Congresses and Inter-Congresses of the World Archaeological Congress.

6. Council

At the time of each Congress of the World Archaeological Congress its Council will comprise one National Representative per country, in addition to the above Regional Representatives and Representatives of Indigenous Peoples/the Fourth World : these National Representatives will be selected by the Individual Member participants from the respective country, and each National Representative will have full voting powers.

Only Council is empowered to elect the President, Secretary and Treasures of the World Archaeological Congress.

At its four-yearly meetings, Council's agenda will also include matters referred to it from regions, Inter-Congresses and from Congress sessions.

One of its main Agenda items will be the arrangements for the next Congress of the World Acrhaeological Congress.

The countries constituting the fourteen Regional ElectoralColleges will be:

1. Central Africa

Angola
Burundi
Cameroon
Central African Republic
Chad
Congo Brazzaville
Equatorial Guinea
Gabon
Rwanda
Zaire

2. Eastern and Southern Africa

Ethiopia
Kenya
Lesotho
Madagascar
Malawi
Somalia
Sudan
Tanzania
Uganda
Zambia
Zimbabwe

3. Northern Africa

Algeria
Egypt
Libya
Morocco
Tunisia

4. Western Africa

Benin
Burkina Faso
Canary Islands
Gambia
Ghana
Guinea
Guinea Bissau
Ivory Coast
Liberia
Mali
Niger
Nigeria
Senegal
Sierra Leone
Togo

5. Central America and the Caribbean

Belize
Caribbean Islands
Colombia
Costa Rica
French Guiana
Guatemala
Guyana
Honduras
Mexico
Nicaragua
Panama
Puerto Rico
Salvador
Surinam
Trinidad and Tobago
Venezuela

6. Northern America

Canada
Greenland
United States of America

7. Southern America

Argentina
Bolivia
Brazil
Chile
Ecuador
Paraguay
Peru
Uruguay

8. Eastern Asia

China
Hong Kong
Japan
Korea
Mongolia
Taiwan
Tibet

9. Southeastern Asia and the Pacific

Australia
Brunei
Burma
Cook Islands
Easter Island
Federated States of Marianas
Fiji
French Polynesia
Hawaii
Indonesia
Kampuchea
Kiribati
Laos
Malaysia
New Caledonia
New Zealand
North Vietnam
Palau
Papua New Guinea
Philippines
Samoa
Singapore
Solomon Islands
South Vietnam
Tavolu
Thailand
Tonga
Vanuatu

10. Southern Asia

Bangladesh
Bhutan
India
Maldive Islands
Mauritius
Ncpal
Sri Lanka

11. Near and Middle East

Abu Dahbi
Bahrain
Iran
Iraq
Israel
Jordan
Kuwait
Lebanon
North Yemen
Oman
Pakistan
Qatar

Saudi Arabia
South Yemen
Syria
Turkey
United Arab Emirates

12. Eastern Europe and Central Asia

Afghanistan
Bulgaria
Poland
Romania
Union of Soviet Socialist Republics

13. Northern Europe

Belgium
Denmark
East Germany
Finland
Iceland
Ireland
Lichtenstein
Luxembourg
The Netherlands
Norway
Sweden
Switzerland
United Kingdom
West Germany

14. Southern Europe

Albania
Andorra
Austria
Czechoslovakia
France
Greece
Hungary
Italy
Monaco
Portugal
San Marino
Spain
Yugoslavia

7 FINANCES

It was agreed that, given the timetable for the proposed World Archaeological Congress organization, the elected executive body should be in post in time for the Waigani Seminar/Inter-Congress of the World Archaeological Congress to be held in Papua New Guinea in September 1988. Nonetheless, there would be problems in the practical execution of the agreed timetable, especially given the shortage of funding. It was felt that sufficient funding should have been achieved through WAC Memberships by the time of the Inter-Congress in order to carry on the administration of voting procedures, and that some funds might have been found to fund at least a proportion of the new executive body to travel to Papua New Guinea. Meanwhile all members of the Steering Committee would continue with their efforts to raise additional funding of *c.* £20,000 (US $36,000) to facilitate the first meetting of the proposed new WAC executive body.

8 Any Other Business

1. It was agreed to write formally to the students who organized the bulk of the protests at the IUPPS meeting in Mainz to congratulate them on raising the debate over academic freedom and apartheid.
2. The Secretary reported on his recent visit to North America as the guest of Ms Hammil and Mr Cruz and reported that a full report by Ms Jane Hubert of their visit would appear in World Archaeological Bulletin 2, but that he wanted to record that the level of feeling by Indian Nations, groups and individuals that he had witnessed about the archaeological investigation of their lives was both genuine and immense.
3. Ms Cane proposed a vote of thanks to the Secretary and to his Secretariat for their efforts over this meeting, which was carried unanimously.

The Meeting closed at 19:00 on 20 October 1987

1. 1 Sanghol : SGL-I, Remains of post-holes on the brick floor.

1. 2 Sanghol : SGL-I, Brick-built rectangular cistern-like structure.

1. 3 Sanghol : SGL-1, Partly exposed Kushana house complex.

1. 4 Sanghol : SGL-2, Late Harappan house plan with mud walls and hearth.

1. 5 Sanghol : Terracotta human figurines.

1. 6 Sanghol : Terracotta human figure, archaic.

1. 7 Sanghol : Female figure on a ceramic handle (Kushana Period)

1. 8 Sanghol : Stamped design of Yaksha on a pot below rim, with design or rim.

1. 9 Sanghol : Terracotta disc stamped with prancing lion and geometric motif on back

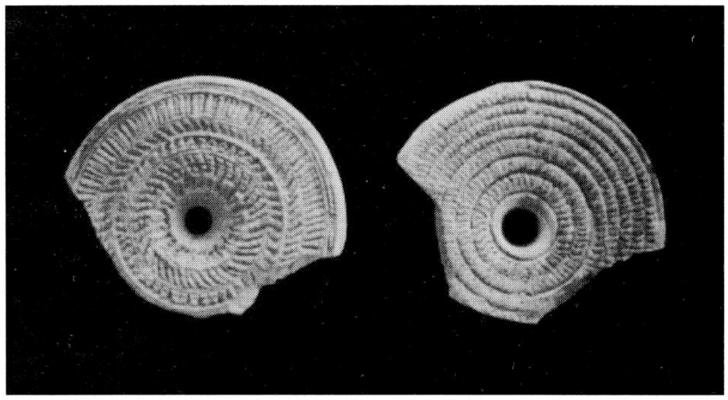

1. 10 Sanghol : Terracotta stamps with handle.

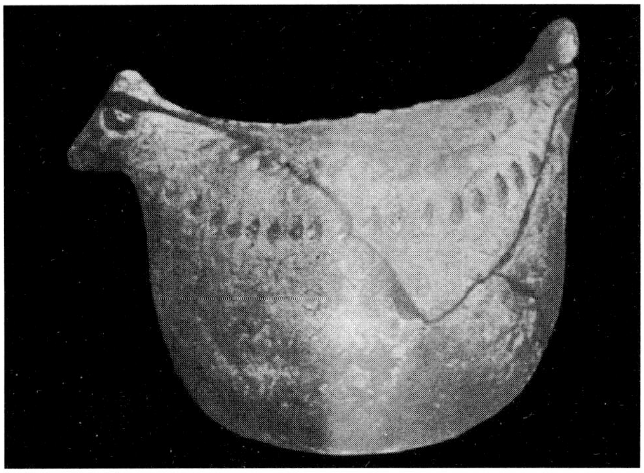

3. 1 Thapli : Painted Grey Ware sherds.

3. 2 Thapli : Terracotta bird.

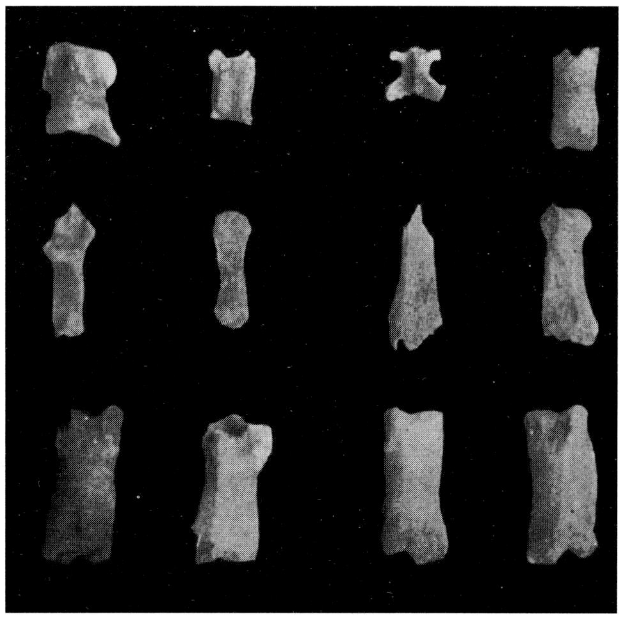

3. 3 Thapli : Faunal remains.

3. 4 Purola : Painted Grey Ware sherds.

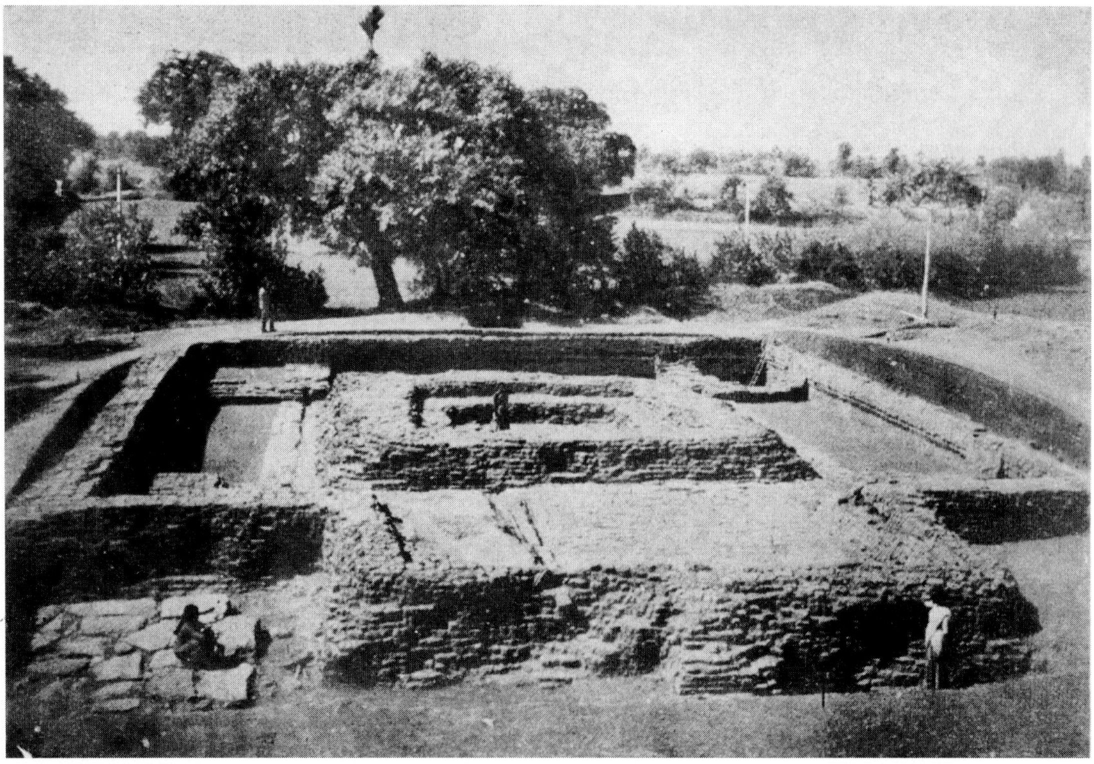

4. 1 Peddavegi : PVG-1, *Stupa* at Dhanamdibba site, Phase IA, Salankayana, 4th century A.D.

4. 2 Peddavegi : PVG-I, Panchayatana complex, Phase-IB, *c.* 5th-6th century A.D.

4. 3 Peddavegi : PVG-II, Paramesvara Temple site, excavated brick temples, Phase-IB, *c.* 5th century A.D.

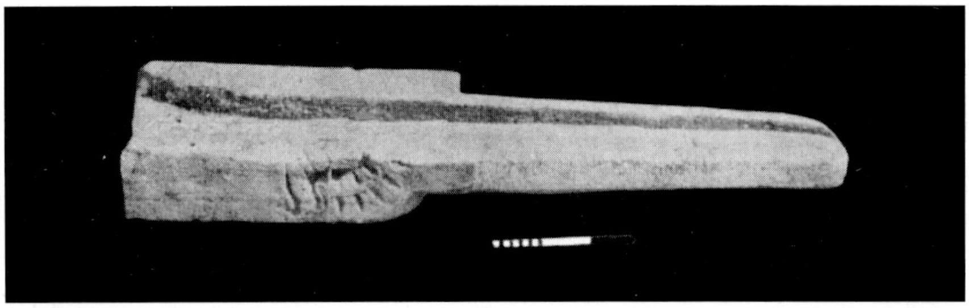

4. 4a Peddavegi : Phase-IB, Inscribed limestone pranala.

4. 4b Peddavegi : Phase IB, Close view of the Inscription-1.

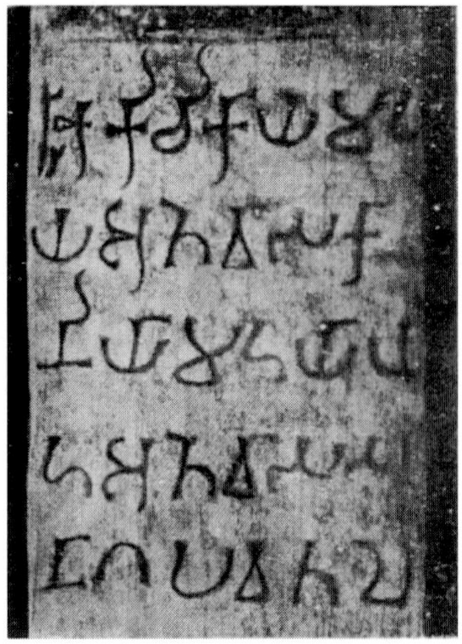

4. 4c Peddavegi : Phase IB, Close view of the Inscription-2.

4. 5a Peddavegi : Phase IA, Siva-Parvati.

4. 5b Peddavegi : Phase IA, Carnelian Intaglio.

4. 6a Peddavegi : Phase IA, Mahishamardini.

4. 6b Peddavegi : Phase IA, Srivatsasakti.

4. 6c Peddavegi : Phase IA, Panchalinga.

4. 6d Peddavegi : Phase IA, Viras.

5. 1 Sannati : Brick building showing platform, rooms, floors, entrances and corridor.

5. 2 Sannati : A view of the brick building from north-east.

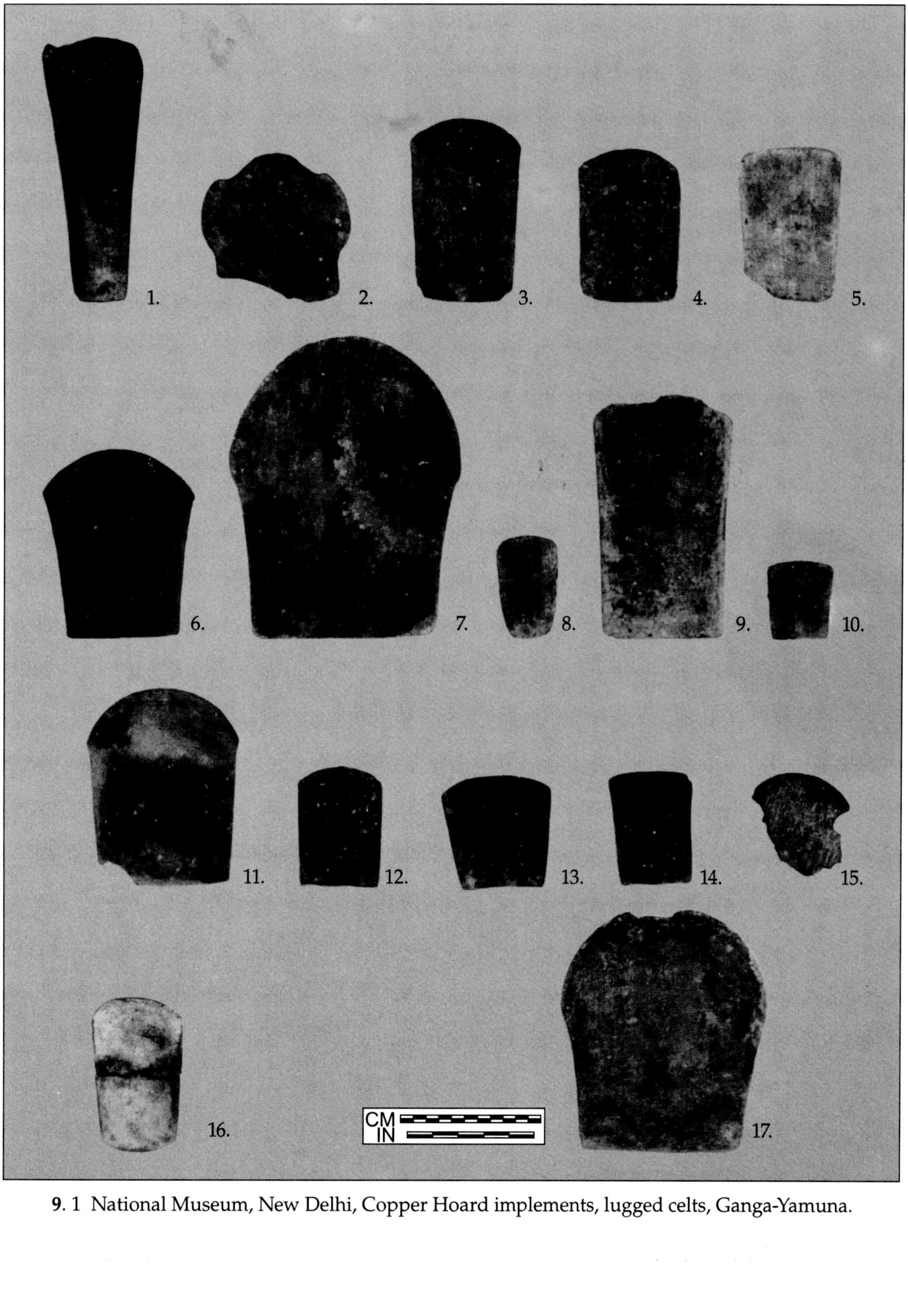

9. 1 National Museum, New Delhi, Copper Hoard implements, lugged celts, Ganga-Yamuna.

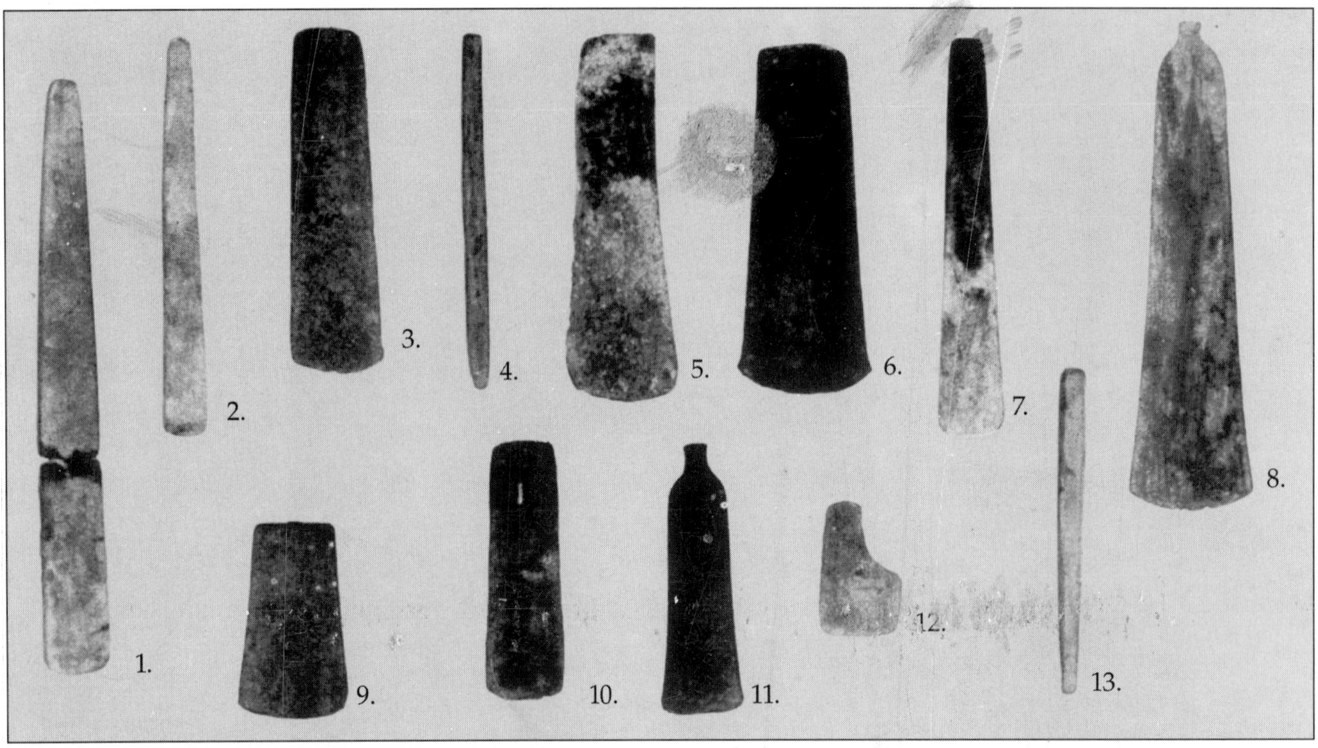

9. 2 National Museum, New Delhi : Copper Hoard implements; Chisels, etc. Ganga-Yamuna doab.

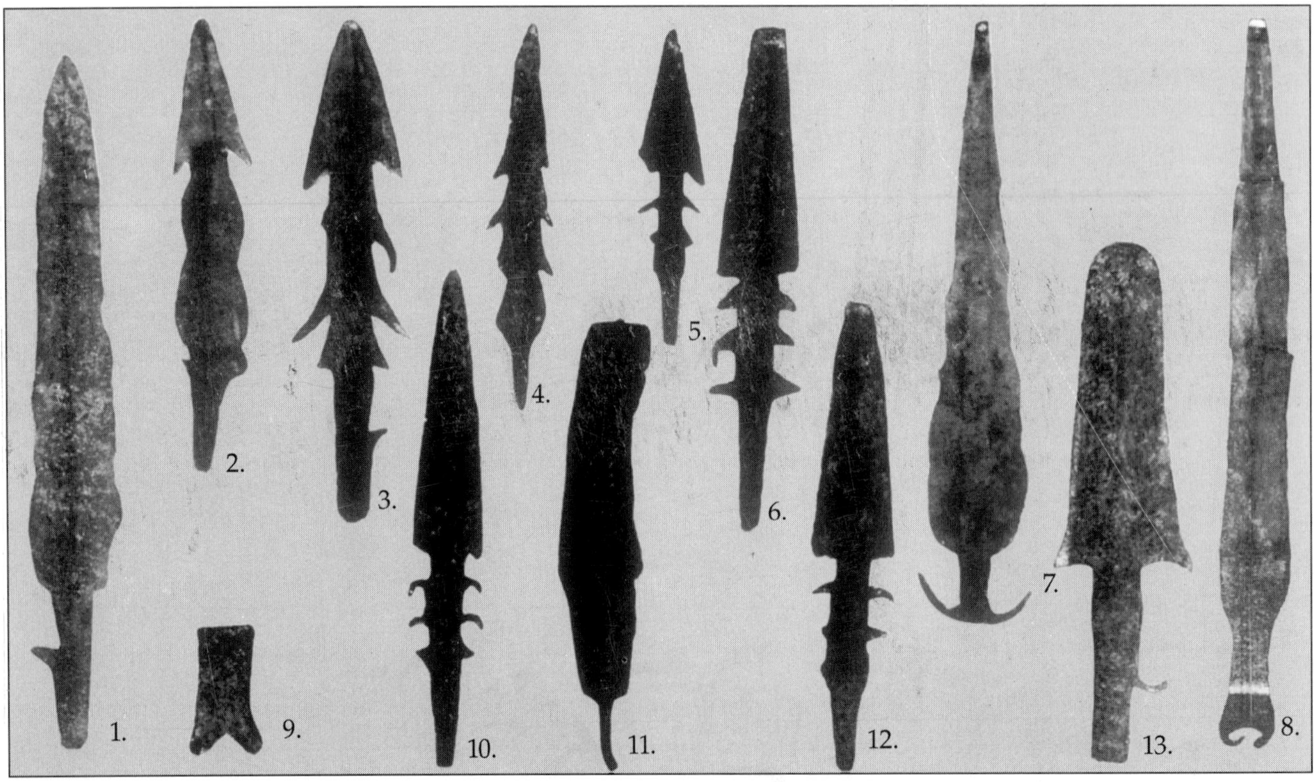

9. 3 National Museum, New Delhi : Copper Hoard implements; harpoons and swords.

11. 1 Fatehpur Sikri : Glazed ware, object C, inner side.

14. 1 National Museum, New Delhi ; Siddhaikavira.

15. 1 National Museum, New Delhi ; Sambhara.